IT USUALLY
BEGINS WITH
AYN RAND

IT USUALLY
BEGINS WITH
AYN RAND

Jerome Tuccille

STEIN AND DAY/*Publishers*/New York

This book is dedicated to deviationists all over the world.

I would like to acknowledge a special debt of gratitude to my editor Renni Browne. Her helpful insights and suggestions along the way have been extremely valuable in the building of this book.

Author's Note

The dialogue that appears throughout these pages should not be taken as a verbatim replay of dialogue which actually took place. On those occasions when I was present, I have attempted to re-create the spirit rather than the precise letter of conversations that transpired. For other incidents, such as those presented in Chapter Two, I have had to rely on information supplied to me by those with firsthand knowledge.

Contents

PART ONE
THE OVERVIEW

1

The Whim Worshipers

It usually begins with Ayn Rand.

The young crusader in search of a cause enters the world of *The Fountainhead* or *Atlas Shrugged* as though he were about to engage in unheard-of sexual delights for the first time. He has been warned beforehand. There is no need to search any further. The quest is over. Here is all the truth you've been looking for contained in the tightly packed pages of two gargantuan novels.

He steps inside, cautiously at first, perhaps even skeptically, but before long he is swept away by the rampaging prose of the author and the heroic activities of her characters. Here are Dominique Francon, newspaperwoman, determined to destroy her man before the altruists can get to him; Howard Roark, architect, designing skyscrapers and dynamiting public housing projects; John Galt, hero par excellence, creating his anarchist utopia in the middle of the Rocky Mountains; Dagney Taggart, beautiful and courageous, running off in a billowing evening gown to save her railroads from extinction; Ragnar Danneskjold, anarchist, blowing up foreign-aid ships on the open seas.

The titles of Rand's nonfiction works give a good indication of the basic tenets of her philosophy: *The Virtue of Selfishness; Capitalism: The Unknown Ideal;* later still, *The Romantic Manifesto.* Ayn Rand was not the first to advocate individualism and economic *laissez faire,* but she was certainly the first to elevate selfishness to the level of a philosophical absolute. To Rand it was simply not enough to believe in individual liberty and the efficacy of the marketplace; you had to have a proper understanding of the fact that altruism is the root cause of all the evil that has ever existed on the face of the earth, and that selfishness (less arrogantly translated into "rational self-interest") is the only proper motivation for all human conduct. All forms of altruism—including voluntary communes and even private charity—are viewed as inherently evil, since they will eventually lead to an altruistic political order: communism, a welfare state, any government designed to promote collective egalitarianism.

For this reason unregulated capitalism is much more than just an efficient economic system to Rand and her followers. It is a moral absolute and the cornerstone of the Randian code of ethics which has its base not in mere voluntarism, but in selfishness in all areas of human activity. Understanding this, it becomes easier to see why the dollar sign is revered by the Randian with the same fervor Christians reserve for the cross, Jews for the star of David, Moslems for the crescent, and middle Americans for Old Glory.

It is all quite heady, this stuff, when fed in massive doses to the impressionable young mind all at once. It is especially appealing to those in the process of escaping a regimented, religious background—particularly young Jews and renegade Roman Catholics, ripe for conversion to some form of religion-substitute to fill the vacuum. The crumbling walls of doctrinaire Catholicism, or heavy-fisted Judaism, leave you with a feeling of vulnerability. Your protective shell is cracking. You're gradually becoming more and more exposed to the great agnostic world out there that the priests and brothers and rabbis have been warning you about since you were five years old. You realize you can't go home again, but where *do* you go?

And then you discover Galt's Gulch at the end of *Atlas Shrugged* and you know everything is going to be all right forevermore. The world is still intact and so are you.

You've become a devout Objectivist.

After eight years of grade-school nuns, four years of prep-school Jesuits, and four more of Christian Brothers in college, I emerged at the end of my formal education with a pronounced distaste for all things papal and divine. Pugnacious, iconoclastic, more libertine than libertarian, I charged into the workaday world in search of icons to smash. Show me anything boasting of security, happiness or certitude in any area, and—wham—I would swing out with my anti-icon stick in an effort to bring it down with a crash. If there was anyone in the Western Hemisphere with a lower resistance to the heady wine of Objectivism, I can't imagine that he or she existed at the time. I later discovered there were legions more like myself back in the early sixties, eager to make the Great Leap— and who actually did, with reckless abandon. For the moment I considered myself unique, a lone and courageous individual who had found the Holy Grail after years of floundering.

Objectivism can be a wonderfully appealing religion substitute for disaffiliated Jews and Catholics from the middle class who turn to it with a mania formerly reserved for their ancestral religion—and also to the sons and daughters of Old American WASPS, brought up on the Protestant ethic of hard work and self-sufficiency. It is a closed system of ideas, even more so than the conservative Catholicism in vogue until the middle sixties. Under the most doctrinaire of Catholic up-bringings there is a certain margin for flexibility. The boundaries are clearly defined, but you are permitted an area of deviation from the straight and narrow before stepping onto the wild shores of heresy. To a lesser extent the same holds true for Judaism.

Not so under the tutelage of the Rand.

Objectivism is an inflexible package deal. Ayn Rand, having established herself as a radical individualist, an uncompromising muckraker and free thinker by the 1950's, then proceeded to erect a tight system of logic embracing every conceivable area of human endeavor. Economics, politics, psychology, child-rearing, sex, literature, even cigarette-smoking—Rand had written about them all, issuing her pronouncements on each subject in turn. Curiously enough, for a woman who started out as a champion of the independent mind, she began to consider her own ideas as natural corollaries of truth and objectivity.

"Objective reality" was what Rand said it was.

"Morality" was conformity to the ethic of Ayn Rand.

"Rationality" was synonymous with the thinking of Ayn Rand.

To be in disagreement with the ideas of Ayn Rand was to be, by definition, irrational and immoral. There was no allowable deviation under the tenets of Objectivism—which, following the publication of Rand's major philosophical novel, *Atlas Shrugged,* in 1957, quickly became a kind of New Marxism of the Right. A generation earlier, the same converts now flocking to her would just as enthusiastically have joined the Marxist band wagon tearing down the rocky road of the thirties. If Marxism, with its promise of a proletarian utopia, was tailor-made to the aspirations of the working-class crusader, Objectivism and its ethic of self-sufficiency and achievement was intoxicating to the sons and daughters of the middle class, graduating from college at the end of the Eisenhower era. The watertight, compartmentalized structure of Randian logic was every bit as self-delineated as that of Karl Marx, condemned by Rand as the paragon of human immorality and depravity. The purges occurring behind the scenes at the Nathaniel Branden Institute, the headquarters of Objectivism, throughout the 1960's were a right-wing replay of Communist Party purges in the 1930's. And deviationism, even today the dirtiest word in the Marxist dictionary, became the cardinal sin for followers of Objectivism.

The dogmatic nature of Objectivism does not become apparent on first contact. Looking back, we can see that a good many people growing up in the 1950's developed a profound disgust for the American *status quo.* The demoralizing atmosphere of the Corporate State, so effectively analyzed by Charles Reich in *The Greening of America,* was already perceived on a subconscious level by many people in the years following the Truman administration. It did not take long to recognize the fact that Eisenhower, rather than charting a new and exciting course that would give people a greater measure of control over the institutions which now dominated their lives, was doing little more than slowing down temporarily our mad rush toward a dictatorship by bureaucracy.

Something was radically wrong with America. There was a feeling in the air, an intimation that we were no longer in control of forces which propelled us faster and faster toward a goal no one had yet been able to define. The American state itself was out of control. This giant apparatus we had come to know as government seemed to be building an inevitable momentum, while operating with a bizarre technocratic intelligence of its own. People with strong opinions on political and social issues ten years before, now shrugged their shoulders as if to say, "What's the use?" "The government" seemed to be running the country with a disembodied intelligence, and even the politicians could do little more than attempt to apply the brakes from time to time.

The world had grown too complicated.

There were forces at work in the world which the average citizen couldn't be expected to understand.

"They"—those hazy and mysterious people in command—had more information than "we the people" did. "They" would see us through all right.

It was comforting to have a benevolent father figure—Dwight D. Eisenhower—at the helm. He was a good man, a just and honest man: a real American. We could trust him to guide us through these confusing times in one piece. We could —we had to—place our future in his hands. He was the father of the American people. He *was* the American people, for Christ's sake! The world was suddenly too big and too complex; the individual's confidence in his ability to conduct the affairs of his own life had shrunk to zero.

The individual *was* a zero, a pygmy, a cipher in the vast machinery of the Corporate State. This was the age of giant bombs, giant nations, corporations, unions; giant and unfathomable political issues. Individualism was obsolete in this era of the Organization Man, the Man in the Gray Flannel Suit, the Suburban Sprawl and the Super Highway. In an era of sameness and conformity, the sacrifice of the individual and his idiosyncrasies to the rigid pattern of the giant American Shopping Center seemed logical. No one was going to rock the boat, to interfere with Father Eisenhower in his divinely ordained task of steering the American nation to safety. Anyone who did was a "Commie," a "Red." He was a goddamned "un-American."

And then along came Ayn Rand.

There was no one more radical than she in championing the autonomy and supremacy of the individual through the rhetoric of her novels. Philosophically, she was a wild and freaky anarchist, an iconoclast, a radical individualist. She created fictional heroes who challenged the authority of Corporate America, who fought the conformity of the American nation-state, who plotted against it and bombed its institutions and brought it down with a resounding crash.

This was the allure of Ayn Rand at the outset—her anarchism, her individualism, her revolutionary radicalism. Ayn Rand said to hell with conformity, to hell with sameness, to hell with Corporate America.

Ayn Rand said "Fuck you!" to Dwight David Eisenhower.

And then, sadly, the seeds of rigidity implanted in her novels bore fruit. This champion of the individual man, of the beauty and variety of the unfettered mind, proceeded to erect her own house of cards. She developed her own system of compartmentalized logic, her own form of religion-substitute, which negated every principle she had established in the abstract such a short time before. Those who flocked to Objectivism for the breath of fresh air it promised in the midst of a choking miasma of political and cultural stagnation soon found themselves trapped in a different kind of intellectual strait jacket—all the more mystifying since it was unexpected.

The ray of hope offered the individual in the basic principles of Ayn Rand's Objectivism was quickly dimmed by its originator. The fact that her original followers could later look back and analyze the "tragic flaw" in her philosophy provided little comfort. It was all the more frustrating because she had given them their first awareness of what they were looking for —and then destroyed her own ideal with narrow vision and ego-crippling rigidity.

Nathaniel Branden had been Rand's chief protégé until he was purged in 1968, ostensibly for "moral depravity," although the real reason was somewhat more personal than that, according to Branden. He had written Rand a fan letter in the early fifties, having decided that *The Fountainhead* was the most "rational" book he had ever read, and his idol was quick to recognize the incisive clarity of his mind.

In view of his obvious brilliance, it was only logical that he be hand-picked by the Rand for private instruction in the rudiments of Objectivism. She even managed to develop him into the second-most-rational-person in the world by the time *Atlas Shrugged* came out in 1957. Branden then created the Nathaniel Branden Institute which immediately went into the business of marketing Rand's philosophy in the form of twenty individual lectures given as a course every spring and fall. Each week the initiate would be treated to a lecture, usually delivered by Branden in his singsong Jewish-Canadian-Northumbrian burr, on a different aspect of Objectivism: Objectivist epistemology; the nature of reason and knowledge; the Objectivist morality; the Objectivist theory of politics and economics; Objectivism and art; Objectivism and literature (presented by Rand herself); Objectivism and psychology, sex—even Objectivism and Aristotle.

Here the novice was plunged headlong into the heady world of second-handers (those who lived primarily off the achievements of others); whim worshipers (those who believed that faith took precedence over reason as a source of knowledge); muscle mystics (those who ruled others by either physical or spiritual intimidation); floating concepts (the application of conceptual knowledge to something other than its source); America's persecuted minority (the U.S. industrialist); A is A (a thing is what it is); altruism (collectivism); collectivism (altruism); the Cult of Moral Grayness (the notion that there are degrees of evil between the extremes of right and wrong);

heroes and heroines (individualists in the *Fountainhead* or *Shrugged* mode); rationalists (those who believed unquestioningly the teachings of Ayn Rand and Nathaniel Branden); thugs, hoodlums, savages, weaklings, and degenerates (those who questioned the teachings of Ayn and Nathaniel Ben Rand).

Until the Institute moved into larger offices in the basement of the Empire State building, these weekly lectures were conducted in the old Sheraton-Atlantic Hotel on Broadway and Thirty-fourth Street in Manhattan. The young student was warned at the outset that it was immoral and improper to call himself an Objectivist until he had taken the basic course at least twice (at seventy dollars per), the advanced course at least once—and, of course, read the entire body of Randian literature and found himself in total agreement with it. He then was formally admitted to the "Senior Collective" comprising a handful of undeviating "individualists." The proper term for all others was "Students of Objectivism," and those outside the Collective who referred to themselves as Objectivists might find themselves marked as second-handers or whim worshipers.

Once agreeing to this basic ground rule, the new student entered the spartan rigidity of the lecture hall determined above all else to prove himself a worthy candidate for the Senior Collective. Each course attracted over a hundred youthful aspirants, all of them convinced that the Law of Natural Selection would propel himself or herself to the top of the heap. There was little smiling or joking as the latest batch of novices, neatly groomed and manicured right down to the last individual, filed past the photographs of Rand and Branden in the anteroom (where student employees carefully checked admittance tickets, ever on the lookout for "frauds and thugs"), past the prominently displayed line-up of Rand's books and officially approved pro-capitalist, anti-collectivist literature, into the main hall with its soldierly rows of straight-back metal chairs.

Smiling, when it happened at all, was indulged in surreptitiously, since humor in the Objectivist handbook was considered immoral and anti-life, a device contrived to destroy man's capacity for greatness; besides, there was little amity among the students to begin with, since they all considered themselves competitors in the race for recognition as fullfledged Objectivists. Admission to the Senior Collective was in fact a kind of Atheists' Armageddon, a sweepstakes competition for capitalistic Jehovah's Witnesses, with the major prizes being awarded for syllogistic rather than spiritualistic perfection. With room at the top for only a chosen few, each student became in effect the enemy of his neighbor; there was very little to smile about.

My first reaction to all of this was awe, the stunned awe of a true-believing convert as devout now in my atheistic capitalism as I had ever been in the baroque Catholicism of the 1950's. Here one was surrounded by a veritable battalion of superior human beings, Galtlike in the no-nonsense jut of their jaws and the drilling determination issuing forth from eyes that never blinked. And heroines galore, many with capes swirling behind them as they swept toward their seats, dollar-sign brooches glinting conspicuously over their hearts, smoking cigarettes through long holders the way Dagney did in *Atlas Shrugged*.

Sweet Jesus! It was so easy to imagine a world populated by such as these, rational and self-sufficient individuals, all conducting their lives in accordance with the Objectivist code: "I swear—by my life and my love of it—that I will never live for the sake of another man, nor ask another man to live for mine." When Branden stepped out—tall, striking, his hair cascading in blond waves over his forehead and eyes sparkling like blue ice—the setting was complete. There wasn't a student in the hall who didn't believe, deep down in the far recesses of his being, that the days of the collectivists—the thugs and hoodlums and irrational muscle mystics—were coming to an end.

Lecture by lecture I found my New Credo slowly beginning to crack. As much as I wanted to believe that the Objectivist package deal held all the answers, the doubts arose one by one until I had no choice but to face them as I had with Catholicism several years before.

Try as I might, I could not swallow whole the idea that altruism was responsible for all the ills afflicting the world of the early 1960's. I saw the issue as a question of individual freedom versus the authority of the state; and the notion that state-corporate monopolies, economic and military imperialism, racism, violence, crime, alienation, etc., all had their roots in an altruistic ethic was too much of a strain even on the most impressionable of mentalities.

My second crisis of conscience revolved around the Randian theory of literature. For someone whose tastes in literature ran the gamut from Hemingway to Maugham to Fitzgerald to Steinbeck to Duerrenmatt to Cheever to Mailer to Salinger to Evelyn Waugh to Perelman to Vonnegut, naturalists and satirists to the last, it was a bit difficult to accept the theory that naturalism and comedy were immoral and anti-life, or that Mickey Spillane and Ian Fleming were the greatest living practitioners of the romanticism of Victor Hugo.

The final straw was the Objectivist theory of sex, a form of atheistic puritanism as severe as that of the most dogmatic Marxist. According to Rand, it was the height of immorality for a man and woman to hop in bed simply because they liked the shape of each other's buttocks. Disciples were permitted carnal bliss only if they were intellectually compatible and shared the same values, the same sense of life, the same moral code.

Rand's analysis of how people were supposed to know when and if they were intellectually compatible had some curious twists. Obviously, lengthy philosophical discussions were extremely time-consuming and distracting, especially if one had an itch to satisfy his sexual needs. No fear. Rand provided students of Objectivism with a short cut. It was not necessary for would-be bedmates to probe each other's psyches at length to determine whether they could make it together or not. Truly rational people had the capacity of recognizing each other *on sight*. Intellectual compatibility, it seemed, could be discerned in the set of someone's jaw or the direct, confident glare of his or her eyes. Rational men and women were invariably tall, beauteous, and lean, with thick, wavy hair, drilling eyes, and strong jutting jaws. This posed a problem for short, dumpy individualists who could practice eye exercises forever, but could never alter their stature and bone structure no matter how hard they tried. From all this one might have assumed the crowning height of ecstasy to be raped on the steps of the New York Stock Exchange by a philosophical heir of William Graham Sumner.

By the time the five-month course was over I had already begun to drift away from the straight and narrow Randian road. The feeling I had experienced back in 1959 when the Dean of Manhattan College warned me of "incipient heresy," skillfully employing the imagery of sizzling flesh and the Pit of Darkness, began to simmer once again.

No matter.

It was always too late to turn back. The time had come to move on to other fields.

The Rational Dancer

2

Behind it all was a search for the libertarian ideal.

While various people had translated the basic principles of libertarianism into differing schools of political philosophy— ranging from radical libertarianism or anarchism to the more conservative variety of libertarianism, in which a government would be created for the sole purpose of providing defense services and a judicial system for its citizens—there were certain fundamental areas in which the most radical and conservative of libertarians could find common ground.

Specifically, a libertarian society was one in which everyone would be free to choose his own life style: to own or not to own property; to work or not to work, for himself or for others; to trade freely in an open market place or not to trade at all; to delineate clearly the boundaries of his own autonomy and live privately, or to join in communes or cooperatives or other communitarian structures on a voluntary basis.

It was a society in which each individual would be free from all attempts at interference in his affairs so long as he

25

did not damage the person or property of anyone else, so long as he did not injure the reputation of others through slander, so long as he did not cheat anyone else by fraud in his dealings with them, so long as he did not pollute the environment with harmful elements, so long as he did not violate the terms of any contract he entered into voluntarily.

It was a society in which each individual had the absolute right to self-defense. This included the right to defend himself against any interference in his own affairs, any violation of his freedom—including violations committed in the name of government.

It was a society in which each individual, acting alone or with others, had the right to structure his social institutions as he saw fit—education, housing, police protection, fire prevention, sanitation, justice, defense, economic relief and welfare, and so on down the list; it was therefore a society in which no one would have the right to tax anyone else against his will to make him support any institutions he didn't believe in.

It was a society in which forcing people to fight for a cause they wanted no part of was unthinkable—the military draft would be considered the severest form of slavery.

It was a society in which all human beings who decided to seek, whether individually or collectively, alternative nongovernmental means of defending their lives and property; alternative means of educating their children, housing their families, insuring themselves against economic hardship, settling their differences with one another; alternative means of doing anything at all which government does for them—would then have the right to withdraw their support from government, to secede from government, to stop sacrificing their lives, property, and taxes to government, to live apart from the jurisdiction of government in a condition of voluntary association.

This was the libertarian society in its most ideal form. These were the values we subscribed to, if only in a vague and hazy form at the time, as we left Manhattan College and points west and continued our search.

From the early 1950's, Murray N. Rothbard, an economist and writer living in New York City, had been one of the most radical and consistent libertarians in the country. He had been an anarchist from his earliest years, subscribing to that school of libertarianism which maintains that all essential services, including military defense and a judicial system, could be provided by an unregulated free-enterprise system without the agency of government.

Rothbard and his close friend, Leonard Liggio, had been active in the' Youth for Taft movement back in 1952. Both were young supporters of what is referred to nowadays as the Old Isolationist Right, the right wing of H. L. Mencken, Garet Garrett, Albert Jay Nock, Frank Chodorov, Leonard Read; the Old Right that used to condemn the liberals for getting the United States involved in overseas adventures such as Korea and even World War II; the Old Right that the New Left started to sound so much like at the beginning of the anti-war movement in 1965.

Rothbard and Liggio also found common ground in the economic theories of Ludwig von Mises, the leading Austrian economist in the United States. They attended the Mises lectures at New York University and then sat around talking afterward in various Greenwich Village cafés, a touch of European intellectual life favored by the Viennese economist. Rothbard's reputation as Mises' chief disciple began to grow in right-wing circles, and he and Liggio (whose field was historical revisionism, another common bond between the Old Right and the New Left of William Appleman Williams and Gabriel Kolko) started to attract a satellite group of their own personal followers. George Riesman, later to become a member of Rand's Senior Collective, was converted to Austrian *laissez faire* primarily through the efforts of Rothbard; Robert Hessen, another budding Objectivist, was a protégé of Liggio's. Others who joined the circle in the middle and late fifties were Ronald Hamowy and Ralph Raico, who founded *The New Individualist Review* to challenge Buckley conservatism in the early 1960's. Another convert was Ed Nash, now the head of his own publishing firm in Los Angeles, whose main interest at that time was establishing a kind of Radio Free Bronx at his home in the University Heights section of that borough. He operated a radio transmitter with a broadcasting radius of about ten city blocks, and eagerly piped right-wing messages to anyone he could reach.

Murray Rothbard had met Ayn Rand around 1950, but they lost contact when Rand moved out to the West Coast for a while shortly afterward. When *Atlas Shrugged* was published in 1957, Rothbard's letter congratulating her on its success got him an invitation to attend the weekly *salons* she was conducting in her apartment in midtown Manhattan.

It was there that Rothbard met Nathaniel Branden and his wife Barbara for the first time. With each gathering the size of the assemblage grew: Ralph Raico, George Riesman, Robert Hessen, and Leonard Liggio were followed by Leonard Peikoff, Alan Greenspan, and Edith Efron. Branden, sensing a profitable supply-and-demand situation in the making, conceived the idea of an institute and a series of public lectures for a fee. It was then and there that the Nathaniel Branden Institute was born.

Through it all, Leonard Liggio remained the least infatuated with the mounting Randian ground swell. From the beginning he detected a kernel of evangelical anti-communism in her thinking that was to give her politics a conservative coloration in the 1960's. He also regarded her historical analysis of the individual roles of the United States and the Soviet Union in world affairs as shallow and unsophisticated. When he discovered that Rand refused even to listen to a more radical interpretation of United States' foreign policy as it had evolved through the first half of the century, whatever interest he had in Rand evaporated altogether.

On Rand's part, she was not sorry to see Liggio's attendance at her weekly *salons* beginning to fall off. For one thing, he was still a practicing Catholic, which could only mean that his basic premises were in a state of degeneration, if not total disrepair. And if that were not enough, he had developed the anti-life habit of falling asleep on her couch whenever she was speaking at any length.

She had no place for hoodlums of that sort in her living room.

The falling away of Murray Rothbard began when the weekly *salons* turned semiweekly. Since it was only logical that rational men and women required the frequent companionship of other rational people to maintain their peace of mind, Rand decided to hold the meetings twice as often. To miss a session for any reason other than death or cataclysmic illness was to commit an irrational and immoral act; it meant you were sacrificing a higher value—conversation with Rand—to a less productive activity.

"Where were you last night, Murray?" Branden inquired by phone the morning after Rothbard missed his first seminar. Branden had added a slight Russian accent to his Canadian-Highland burr, possibly an unconscious assimilation of Rand's vocal pattern.

"I was tired, Nathan. I decided to stay home and get some sleep."

"You were tired? You were too tired to discuss the philozophical development of muzzle mystizism in the thirteenth and fourteenth zenturies?"

"I didn't get any sleep the night before, Nathan. I just couldn't make it."

"I zee. I zuppose I will just have to tell Ayn that Murray

Rossbott was too tired to attend her Tuesday *salon*. Is *that* what you want me to do?"

"Well I suppose so. I mean, it's the truth."

"I zee. You will be along tomorrow night of course?"

"Sure, I'll be down."

"We look forward to zeeing you."

Shortly afterward, it became known that Rothbard's wife, Joey, was a devout Protestant, a practicing Christian who actually believed that faith and altruism had a positive moral value. When the last tremors caused by this revelation finally faded away, a pall of silence fell over the living room. There was a Christian in the house. Not a renegade Christian who acknowledged the sins of her past and was ready to make amends for them. Not an apostate Christian who had forever forsaken the principles to which she formerly adhered. But a real, live, breathing Protestant who admitted belief in the existence of a Supreme Being! A heretic such as this was occupying the armchair in Ayn Rand's living room. And was married to one of Rand's most gifted protégés, no less, who now sat beside her with a look of villainous unconcern on his face.

Well, if Murray Rothbard's wife was a Christian there could only be one logical explanation for it: she had obviously never read Ayn Rand's proof that a Supreme Being does not, did not, will not, and could not exist. Ever.

Branden hustled her into an adjoining room and sat her down at a desk with a handful of Rand's anti-God essays. Joey, relieved to be out of earshot of all this talk of second-handers and floating concepts, pored over the pamphlets while the meeting continued in the other room. When she completed her assignment and returned to the gathering, the drone of conversation suddenly stopped and she found herself skewered by some twenty pairs of drilling eyes.

Branden took the initiative. "Well?"

"I found it all very interesting, Nathan."

"She found it very interezting," Branden repeated the information to the others at no extra charge. "Anything elze?"

"The arguments are very good, but I'm still not an atheist if that's what you're getting at."

Rand decided to take over. This was unquestionably a matter that demanded her personal intervention. "You haf read ze proofs?"

"They're all very good and thought-provoking, Ayn. But you don't shake a lifetime of religious faith with a few articles. I'll have to think about it for a while."

"You haf read ze proofs and you ztill inzist on wallowing in your mindless myztizizm? Faith is irrational which means. . . ."

"Which means zat faith is immoral," said Branden.

"Which means it is anti-life," said Peikoff.

"Which means it is anti-man," said Hessen.

"Which means it is anti . . . anti . . ." said Barbara Branden, searching for a suitable phrase.

"Enoff!" said Rand, clapping her hands. "Zere has been enoff zmall talk for vun night. Do you haf anymore questions to ask me?"

This was the signal that the meeting was adjourned for the night. No. No one had any questions. Ayn was getting a headache. It was time for everyone to go home.

This incident marked the beginning of the end of Murray Rothbard's eminent position in the Objectivist hierarchy. He, like Liggio, had begun to question the wisdom of many Randian attitudes on political and, particularly, historical affairs. He compounded his crime of being happily married to a practicing altruist at the following meeting when he refused, at the insistence of Rand and Branden, to leave his wife and take a more rational mate. There were any number of Dagney

Taggart types, complete with capes, cigarette holders, and dollar-sign brooches, whom he might have considered.

Shortly afterward there was a meeting at which he found himself denounced for not smoking cigarettes. Cigarettes were pro-life and pro-man since they were manufactured by productive capitalists for human enjoyment; to be against tobacco on the grounds that it was destroying your lungs was to be against the creative efforts of industrialists who had gone through all their trouble for consumers who didn't appreciate what was being done for them. It was a paradigmatic case of ingratitude at the very least; an argument could even be made that it was immoral.

Then there was the *salon* at which everyone rose individually, Alcoholics Anonymous style, and gave a brief testimonial on the one person in their lives who had made the greatest impact.

"Ayn Rand has influenced me most because . . ."

"The one person who has affected me most was Ayn Rand. This woman more than anyone else . . ."

"The writings of Ayn Rand have opened new horizons . . ."

And so it went around the circle until one young fellow stood up and said, "The person who had the greatest influence on my life was Rocco Fantozi. Rocco helped . . ."

Branden leaped to his feet. "Who in bloody hell is Rocco Fantozi?!"

"Why, he was a friend of mine in high school. When I was sixteen I had a rough period after my parents got a divorce, and Rocco pulled me through. I don't think . . ."

Needless to say, he was purged on the spot.

By this time Rothbard had about had his fill. In addition to everything else that had taken place, he was tired of hearing his name pronounced "Rossbott" all the time. There was some excuse for the Russian-born Rand, but none at all for Branden, born and raised in a predominantly English-speaking country, notwithstanding his eclectic and variegated accent.

Around this time a slick Latino from Brooklyn who gave dancing lessons at Don Pallini's or Fred Astaire's or some similar emporium discovered Rand and declared himself in total agreement with her ideas. Rand was immediately taken by the sheen of his hair and the rapier-like keenness of his mind. Having already decided it was immoral for true Objectivists to socialize voluntarily with nonbelievers, she now decided that the cha-cha, tango, mambo, and samba were the highest social skills yet developed by Western Man. When she entreated him to teach his terpsichorean arts to the rest of the Senior Collective, Murray Rothbard decided to bid farewell. The addition of a Rational Dancer to the Senior Collective was more than he could take.

The climax to this crucial episode in American history came in the summer of 1958. Since it was unthinkable for anyone to leave the Randian nest of his own accord, an emergency meeting of the Senior Collective was called to hear the various charges of deviationism that had been compiled against Rothbard over the past six months. Leonard Liggio was offered the chance to sit in and register his own vote, but he missed his opportunity for moral redemption by dismissing the affair as "silly and unimportant."

The vote to purge Rothbard from the World of Reason was not unanimous but, alas, Riesman and Hessen, former protégés of Rothbard and Liggio from an earlier time, cast their votes with the majority—as they did ten years later when Branden's turn finally came and he, too, was ejected from the world he had worked so hard to create.

3

With a Jaw Like That
He Can't Lose

Those libertarians disillusioned with Ayn Rand and her Objectivism were left, for the time being, without a home of their own. There were others in the country who felt the way they did, of course. You knew about them because you exchanged letters with them once in a while, and you came across their articles now and then in some obscure journal no one else had ever heard of. Their ideas were usually buried in an avalanche of ponderous tracts on economic theory—the ones that were sprinkled throughout with mathematical formulae and technical language that gave you a headache if you read them too carefully. Or else they were mimeographed on those defective little machines with pale blue ink and broken letters which made you squint for hours afterward.

It was a time of disillusionment and uncertainty. And frustration, because you knew things were getting worse instead of better. Somehow you had been caught between generations. Having gone to school in the age of Pat Boone, Johnny Ray, and Dwight D. Eisenhower, you'd come along too late to be fully a part of the Beatnik world of Jack Kerouac, Lawrence

35

Ferlinghetti, and Allen Ginsberg. By the late 1950's the Beat-nik subculture was already on the wane, and cool, progressive jazz—the one medium you could really understand and call your own—was rapidly leaving the American continent for Paris and London. The age of flower children and Rock music was a few years away, and by the time it got going you would be a little too old to identify with the under-twenty-five youth subculture anyway.

Adrift as you were—culturally, generationally, politically—you entered the decade of the sixties convinced that the world would never last another five years. Sooner or later the Bomb would go off. It didn't matter, really, who dropped the first one, the Russians or ourselves. The general effect would be the same. Death, destruction, radioactive clouds all over the whole planet. *On the Beach* was real. It was only a question of how much longer. The Bomb was so big and out of control, so far beyond the reach of you, the individual. There was nothing you could do about it. Shrug your shoulders and dismiss it all with a hopeless gesture. Invest your life savings in a fallout shelter for the back yard, next to the barbecue pit. There was little reason for optimism.

If, miraculously, the powers that be managed to control their paranoia and restrain themselves from totally destroying the earth, there was still no doubt that American society was in an imminent state of collapse. The death throes had already begun, the final hours were now at hand. The Presidential election of 1960 was proof enough of that. To the libertarian, John F. Kennedy typified everything that had been wrong with the corporate, liberal, technocratic elite for nearly thirty years. If elected, he would move into Washington with an army of think-tank intellectuals and pragmatic social engineers to dictate a scientistic policy that would touch every conceivable area of human activity. No stone would be left unturned, no corner of the country free of regulation from the social planners in

Washington. Nineteen sixty-one could be 1984 before its time.

On the other hand, Richard M. Nixon was a thoroughly inadequate opponent from a libertarian viewpoint. He had been a sorry figure under Eisenhower, representing the worst aspects of conservatism—obsessive anti-Communist hysteria—without any noticeable traces of real economic and civil libertarianism. He seemed capable only of me-tooing the state-corporate programs of the Kennedy liberals, instead of challenging the basic concepts themselves. By parroting the Kennedy nostrums about what must be done to save American society, stipulating only that somehow *he* could implement them more effectively, he offered no philosophical opposition to the liberal elitism of J.F.K.

Oh, if somebody pressed you to it, you admitted reluctantly that you did prefer Nixon to John F. Kennedy. But it certainly was not a strong enough preference to prod you into the polling booth.

You didn't even bother to vote that year.

In the midst of your disillusionment and frustration, in the midst of this cultural and political and philosophical vacuum in which you found yourself adrift, a storyland politician—the likes of whom you had never seen before—suddenly and unexpectedly stepped into the spotlight. Who was he? What was he saying? Could it be that an American politician was actually saying things like that at this time and in this place? It was overwhelming. It was too much to be believed.

It was time for Barry Goldwater.

Barry Goldwater was a Randian character with a jaw like Barry Goldwater's. One look at him and you knew he belonged in Galt's Gulch, surrounded by striking heroes with blazing eyes and lean, dynamic heroines with swirling capes.

In building the characters for her books, Rand invariably described the altruists as flabby men with shifty eyes, poor muscle tone, and names like Ellsworth Toohey or Wesley Mouch; the egoists, of course, were beauteous and tall and their names, when spoken, rang with the hardness of steel and granite. This was a built-in absurdity in Rand's fictional characterizations which exposed her to a great deal of criticism from both the Left and Right. Her either-or philosophy and Goldwater's no-compromise political attitudes were ready-made to dovetail with each other in an era when "pragmatism" was the order of the day, absolutism and consistency were out, compromise and relativistic problem solving were in; when anyone who believed in a firm and consistent set of principles was regarded as single-minded or shallow.

But by reducing consistency of principle to the level of a Hegelian dialectic, Rand committed an error in reverse logic. Rereading *The Fountainhead* and *Atlas Shrugged* with the benefit of hindsight, one can see that this either-or distinction Rand creates—most obviously through her characterization— laid the groundwork for a similar Hegelian dialectic when she developed her political philosophy. Man is *either* hero *or* villain; he is *either* good *or* bad; he is *either* tall, lean, and heroic *or* short, squat, and villainous.

By the time Goldwater appeared on the scene, Rand had already embraced the Cold War dialectic which translated into: it's *either* the United States *or* the Soviet Union; if we are the apotheosis of virtue they become, by definition, the embodiment of evil. Rand's error in challenging the pragmatism and anti-absolutism of her era is the old one of tossing out the baby with the bath water: if compromise and day-to-day problem solving is wrong, then a black-and-white, either-or value structure must be right. Consequently there can be no such thing as shades of gray, no such thing as degrees of good and evil. It was therefore all but inevitable that her Hegelian code would translate into political conservatism in the Cold War era. Since she had selected the United States over the Soviet Union, that choice necessarily shaped her politics in terms of a struggle between the United States and the Soviet Union locked in irreconcilable conflict. The notion that each side might be partially right *and* partially at fault was unthinkable.

At the same time there was no question that this dichotomous imagery appealed to many libertarians, especially those who tended to view the world in Darwinist terms. Social Darwinism—particularly the survival-of-the-fittest syndrome—has always had a strong influence on the individualist Right.

When Goldwater's *The Conscience of a Conservative* came out in 1960, it naturally found its mark with many of the same people who had already been turned on by *The Fountainhead* and *Atlas Shrugged*. There was a strong libertarian undercurrent running through the book, with the same disgust for the expanding Corporate State and its totalitarian tendencies that was dramatized in Ayn Rand's novels. And the either-or anti-communism of Goldwater meshed almost perfectly with the Objectivist logic. But more important than his message was the fact that Goldwater managed to *look the part* as though he had been made for it.

He was from the Southwest, still a frontier area in many respects. He was tall, well set up and ruggedly youthful in his middle age. He looked better in jeans and rawhide than he did in ties and suits. And that jaw! Jumping Jesus on roller skates, his jaw could have been chiseled by Rand herself. It was perfect. So strong and hard and it stuck out just the right amount. No one else in the country had one quite like it. Things would never have been the same had *The Conscience of a Conservative* been written by a fat, balding man with cigar ashes dribbling down his shirtfront.

Nor would the book have had the same impact had it been written by an author named Wesley Mouch. Wesley Mouch, individualist, somehow wouldn't have made it. But Barry Goldwater! Barry, by itself, was a bit swishy perhaps; but when coupled with Goldwater? The last name was perfection. *Gold,* with all its connotations of hard currency and the free market. And Gold*water?* It rippled, it shone, it glittered. The combination was dynamite. Students all over the country who hated the Corporate State and wanted to see it replaced by an individualistic way of life were freaked out by Goldwater. There was no one else like him.

Rand and then Goldwater, in fact, seemed to offer the only real alternatives to the American Corporate State. There was no one else. *Atlas Shrugged* had hit a certain segment of the American political and cultural consciousness with the impact of a lightning bolt. For all its flawed imagery and comic-strip characterizations, it was the first revolutionary outcry against the unbearable *status quo* of Organization-Man America to come along, the first truly radical critique and denunciation of the Leviathan U.S. power structure. Two years later, along comes Barry Goldwater, a hero straight from the pages of *Atlas Shrugged.* The combination and timing couldn't have been more effective had the whole thing been staged by a Hollywood press agent.

It is probably safe to say that without the one-two punch of the Rand-Goldwater assault on American consciousness, the New Left radicalism of the middle 1960's would have taken a different form entirely. The initial anarchism of the New Left in its earliest days owes much of its basic formulation to the Rand-Goldwater inheritance. Their anti-establishmentarianism was admired by many of the original leaders of the New Left such as Tom Hayden and Carl Oglesby, even as they rejected the anti-communism and free-market economics of Rand and Goldwater. Without this burst of anarchistic individualism in the early sixties, the radical Left uprisings against the political structure would have been more closely bound up in the state socialist and Marxist concepts of the Old Left. The gradual dissipation of libertarian forces in the New Left movement may be largely attributed to the failure of Rand and Goldwater to come up with a consistent libertarian alternative. To put it another way, the basic flaws in the Rand-Goldwater brand of libertarianism may have planted the seeds for the dissolution of libertarian elements in the New Left movement that was shortly to follow.

When he ran for President in 1964, the enthusiasm surrounding Goldwater's candidacy exceeded that of the McCarthy youth movement that would come in 1968. A mania had gripped those of us who supported him. He was more than just a candidate; he would be more than just a President. He was literally hero-worshiped by his followers, embodying as he did everything we held sacred. His philosophy seemed quasi-Randian, but he was a *politician*—potentially a powerful one. And unlike other politicians, he would never compromise with the pragmatists and knee-jerk problem solvers in Washington. He epitomized the free market, self-sufficiency, and a style of life that was being eroded a little bit more each day.

He had to win, there were no two ways about it. Everything was at stake. If he lost, it would mean a return to the same old crap for another four-year period. Four more years of L.B.J., of the Great Society. Barry would change all that. We never considered for one moment that his will would be stymied by a recalcitrant Congress. All he had to do was drill those flabby, compromising Congressmen with his ice-blues and the opposition would dissolve before him.

The first trepidations began to set in during the early stages of the campaign. Who was advising the man? Who was conducting his battle for the Presidency?

"Did you hear what Goldwater said last night?"

"No. What?"

"No more farm subsidies. To an audience in the middle of Kansas, no less."

The day before, he had told a Golden Age Club gathering

that Social Security would have to go. A week earlier he was calling for an end to import quotas—before a group of oil magnates. If it wasn't that, he was telling white Mississippians that black people had the same rights they did. Or pacifists that we had to defoliate the jungles of southeast Asia.

"What's the matter with him?"

"He's dumb."

"He's crazy."

"He's not dumb, he's just honest. He's got *principles,* for Christ's sake!"

"Principles don't win elections."

If only he would keep his mouth shut. If only he would just walk around and let people look at his jaw! With a jaw like that he didn't have to say anything.

Now L.B.J. was beginning to cut into his physiognomy vote. Some people were beginning to suggest that L.B.J. looked a little like John Wayne. Oh my God, not John Wayne! John Wayne was one of ours. Why the hell couldn't Goldwater be running against somebody like Adlai Stevenson? Stevenson didn't look like John Wayne. Stevenson looked like an altruist. Adlai Stevenson looked like Wesley Mouch.

Barry Goldwater would have been a shoo-in against Adlai Stevenson.

When it was over the whole world had fallen in. John Galt had been buried in a landslide. It was overwhelming. It was incredible. The American voter was incorrigibly irrational. The fabric of American society was corrupt and rotten all the way through. Ragnar Danneskjold had the right idea. You had to blow the whole system sky-high. That was the only way to get rid of it. No more of this crapping around with elections and reform. No more bullshit. Reform within the system was impossible.

Goldwater was dead. Howard Roark, John Galt, and Hank

Reardon had been rejected by an overwhelming majority of
the American people. Sixty-five percent of the population was
degenerate and anti-life. Galt's Gulch receded further away into
the clouds. There would never be an opportunity like this
again.

Overnight, a reaction against Goldwater began to set in
among his supporters. He let us down. He had all the right
ingredients—a jaw, a name, a book—and he blew it. He was
a phony hero, a fake. He didn't belong in the same league as
John Galt. He was an imposter, a whimworshiping second-
hander, a muscle mystic. He was a tin hero with mixed premises. And he was also a religionist. His inconsistencies stuck
out like warts all over his face. If you took a closer look you
could detect a certain shiftiness about the eyes. There was a
weakness there which belied the strength and hardness of his
jaw.

If only Nathaniel Branden had run for President instead of
Goldwater. There was a man whose consistency on every basic
issue was incontestable. Or Ayn Rand, for that matter. The
first woman President of the United States.

But both of them were born outside the country. Only a
native American could run for the highest office. There was
no one else. After Goldwater, there simply was no one else to
turn to.

Reform within the system was impossible. That left only one
alternative. Dare one say the word? It ran against the grain of
the whole conservative frame of mind. And yet . . .

Ragnar Danneskjold! Where were you now that we needed
you more than ever?

4

The Impact of
Ivy League Hegelianism

William F. Buckley, Jr. had never really turned us on that much. His appeal to the right-wing mentality had never been primarily libertarian in nature, despite the fact that in his earliest days he had often jokingly referred to himself as an anarchist.

In 1965, he emerged as an active political candidate for the first time, raising high the banner of the Conservative Party in his race for the Mayoralty of New York City. You campaigned openly for him, mainly because you lived in the city and wanted life there to be as agreeable as possible while you did, and you saw no hope in either of the two major candidates. John Lindsay, the Republican nominee, was an unimaginative corporate-liberal on the order of Jacob Javits, representing a point of view which was anathema to your own, and Abraham Beame was the candidate of the conservative-populist Democratic Party with a tradition of subsidizing the city's monopolistic, racist, blue-collar trade unions. The war in Vietnam was not yet the crucial issue it was to become a year or two later, so you found yourself supporting Buckley despite the fact that his brand of Rightism was becoming, every day, more obviously different from your own.

Back in the early 1950's, when Buckley had hit the country with *God And Man At Yale,* his conservative philosophy was peppered throughout with a generous dash of libertarianism. In the beginning, the terms libertarian and anarchist held no shock value for him personally, and he delighted in using both of them to describe that part of his philosophy which advocated economic *laissez faire* and personal freedom from government intervention. He found common ground in the thinking of such Old Right libertarians as Albert Jay Nock and Frank Chodorov, whose philosophies ranged from total anarchism to a radical form of severely limited government. "The amount of government I believe in would fit inside my kitchen," was a favorite slogan of Chodorov's.

Buckley, in the beginning, was able to incorporate this type of anarchistic individualism into his own philosophy and to espouse it with an apparent degree of sincerity. Within a short time, however, it became obvious that there was another side to the Buckley mentality, a side which contradicted and was at total variance with his libertarianism, a side which was later to grow and dominate the other until the remaining elements of libertarianism in his thinking were reduced to little more than weak rhetoric. The dominant anti-libertarian side of Buckley's conservatism can best be described as crusading, even evangelical anti-communism.

The Hegelian dichotomy in Buckley's mentality presented itself in the following manner: simultaneously, he held two irreconcilable premises to be absolute truths. The first stated that the individual had the right to remain free from all outside intervention in his life so long as he conducted his affairs in a nonaggressive manner. This was libertarian philosophy, pure and simple. The second premise stated that the existence of atheistic communism was the single greatest evil mankind faced on earth, and that a powerful American nation-state was the only effective means of protecting our Western heritage from destruction by this insidious Red menace. This, of course, was the conservative anti-Communist side to the Buckley mentality which was to become increasingly dominant throughout the balance of the fifties and the decade to follow.

He attempted to maintain this precarious balancing act between a call for unobtrusive government, and a strong nation-state with a large, powerful, and aggressive government existing only to combat the "Red disease" in the international arena, while maintaining at the same time a hands-off policy in domestic affairs. When he later realized that this concept was an impossible dream—primarily because a large military establishment depends heavily on a military draft and high taxation, profoundly anti-libertarian measures—he was forced to readjust his political formulation and speak of the "temporary suspension of individual liberties" until international Communism could be defeated. By the middle 1950's the escalation of Buckley's conservative anti-Communist philosophy and the de-escalation of his individualist libertarianism was well under way.

Having solved this Hegelian dilemma to his own satisfaction, he was able to concentrate more thoroughly on the development of a sophisticated intellectual foundation for his anti-Communist conservatism. Since he had now reconciled the libertarian-conservative dialectic by "temporarily" suspending most libertarian goals, it was now possible for him to live with such measures as a "temporary" military draft, "temporary" confiscatory taxation, and "temporary" abridgment of civil liberties at home to support a large "temporary" anti-Communist, militaristic nation-state. He would have preferred to have Americans *voluntarily* give themselves—bodily, spiritually, and monetarily—to the creation of an anti-Communist juggernaut.

This would have enabled him to eat his cake and have it at the same time, to have a *voluntary* slave state without having to violate what remained of his libertarian sensibilities. But if Americans were too unsophisticated to realize that a condition of "temporary servitude" was actually in their own best interests, why then it became necessary to save them from their wrongheadedness despite themselves.

It was their own fault, goddamnit!

If the people were too stupid to realize what was good for them, it wasn't Buckley's fault, was it? He was willing to give them a chance to flock to the banner of the Crusades. If the foolish creatures couldn't understand that the "moral climate" of Western society was being eroded a little bit more every day by insidious heresies, somebody had to see that the proper measures were taken to safeguard their traditions.

Of course, all this was interwoven with religious considerations. Buckley was reflecting an attitude that has long been prevalent, not only in Western society but throughout the world. Over the centuries the institutions of religion and government have somehow become inseparable. There has never been a true "separation of church and state" on a practical level. Men have merely transferred their devotion to God and religion to the institution of government. The "Divine Right to Rule" is still very much a part of the psychological make-up of most human beings. There have been few patriots who did not believe in—and who were not willing to risk their lives to defend—the concept that God was on the side of their particular nation-state. "God" is simultaneously "on the side of" the Germans, the Italians, the French, the Japanese, and the Americans even as they butcher one another. No man has ever died for his "country" alone, and very few men have ever died to defend their "freedom." Most men who go willingly to war have believed, very strongly, that they were fighting "God's cause."

Understanding this, we begin to see a little more clearly why so many Americans have waxed violent over the so-called issue of flag desecration. What is being spat or shot upon is not merely a piece of cloth with red and white stripes and white stars on a blue background; it is "God's face" that is being bombarded; Jesus on the cross who is being trampled underfoot. And so the overlay of the peace symbol on the flag is considered "desecration," while the superimposition of a B-52 on the same flag is regarded as "patriotic." Bigger and Better Bombs for Jesus might well be the rallying cry of our present crop of American super-patriots who see the American nation-state as the sacred repository of Western religious traditions. Nuke the Reds and Bomb Hanoi! Rape the earth in the name of Christ!

Consciously or not, the highly sophisticated Buckley began to appeal to these unsophisticated attitudes in the pages of *National Review,* which he founded in 1955 with the financial and editorial assistance of a wide range of intellectuals and writers on the Right. Many libertarians, such as Frank Chodorov and Murray Rothbard, joined forces with *National Review* at first, then later severed relations with it to protest the increasingly hawkish and authoritarian coloration of Buckley's politics. It is interesting to look back at certain factors underlying the rising influence, at the time, of Buckley conservatism in right-wing circles, and the concomitant loss of influence suffered by the Old Right libertarians.

The Old Right with all its positive elements—its instinctive distrust of political power, its mind-your-own-business attitude on foreign policy—also carried with it a history of provincial anti-intellectualism and, in some quarters, a strain of anti-Semitism. These characteristics of the Old Right mentality were long a target of abuse for perhaps the most intellectual Rightist of the 1930's and 1940's, H. L. Mencken. "Booboisie" and "Boobus Americanus" were two of the choice epithets he used to describe such attitudes. By the late 1940's the term "Neanderthal" had all but become a synonym for "Right-Wing Republican," and, in many instances, with fairly good justification.

Buckley's rapid rise through the right-wing hierarchy must be seen against the background of this intellectual vacuum. The more sophisticated types on the Right—students, journalists, academicians—were desperate for a leader of sufficient stature to come along and do battle on their behalf. Buckley was tailor-made to fit the role. He was a Northeastern intellectual and a graduate of Yale, of all places, a major crucible for the formulation of the liberal point of view. He was urbane and eloquent; he had wit; he had charm; he was everything the conservatives had come to associate with liberalism in every respect except one: his ideology. On that point he was one of their own, a philosophical conservative. So great was the intellectual inferiority complex of the Right by this time that the average conservative could do nothing but hero-worship a fellow Rightist who epitomized, in most areas, the thing they themselves feared most—the image of the liberal intellectual. These Buckley qualities, combined with his timely entry into the public arena, were prime factors in his quick ascension to a position of prominence on the Right. Had he been a liberal, he would have been lost in the lines of candidates already forming up for the New-Frontier, Great-Society regimes of the 1960's.

Once he had established himself as the Golden Boy of the New Right, it was then only a question of how he would maintain his pre-eminent position. By the end of the 1950's, William F. Buckley and *National Review* had come to be recognized as the major voice of conservatism in the United States. There was certainly no shortage of libertarian intellectuals attempting to subvert the mounting Buckley influence on the Right during this period. Through the late 1950's and early

1960's, they kept up a steady barrage of articles designed to reaffirm the decentralist principles of the Old Right and detour the New Right from its steady march toward a hawkish foreign policy. But with all the flak and all the intramural squabbles he found himself in, Buckley managed to build his base and increase his influence during a period beginning around 1953 and extending all the way through the next decade.

When you look back, the reasons are not hard to see. First, no one else on the Right was as successful as William Buckley in doing battle with the common enemy—the hated liberal intellectual. He could jab, feint, hook, and counterpunch with the best of them, and he had an uncanny gift for detecting an opponent's hidden weaknesses and driving in the shaft at the most opportune moment. For this ability he was rewarded with the unquestioning admiration of an appreciative right-wing audience—much the same as Adam Clayton Powell, once he had established himself as an expert gadfly capable of ruffling the white man's composure, could do no wrong in the black community.

It was also true that our religious traditions—particularly the Christian tradition—were of great importance to conservatives in the 1950's and the first half of the 1960's, and the Left was regarded as the major destroyer of religious morality in the United States. Consciously or not, Buckley was able to parlay this fear of atheism and other "un-American doctrines" into a source of power for himself. He and his cohorts at *National Review* had seen this atheistic menace—exemplified in communism—for what it was, and they would do everything in their power to save the nation from it. William F. Buckley was, in fact, seen by his constituency as the final barrier between everything they considered holy and the barbaric reach of the antichrist (communism) which threatened to engulf the earth.

By the time Buckley emerged as a political candidate in

the New York mayoralty race of 1965, his brand of conservatism was already unacceptable to a great many libertarians. And yet there simply was no one else to turn to. To libertarians, Lindsay and Beame represented an even more alien philosophy than Buckley. In the wake of the Goldwater disaster of 1964, you had given up almost all hope for libertarian reform within the system. Buckley was bad, but the others were worse. Maybe, just maybe, your candidate would rediscover some of his old libertarian principles of years before and implement them, even on a limited scale, in New York City. Maybe he would demunicipalize the Sanitation Department or decentralize the school system or decontrol the housing situation. Maybe. That would be something at least, wouldn't it?

There was nothing else to hope for, no one else to turn to. Your options were becoming more and more limited all the time.

5

Please Don't Kill
Lenny Bruce

Buckley's defeat in the New York City mayoralty race of 1965 was considerably less traumatic than Goldwater's demise the previous year. For one thing, he had entered the contest more as a gadfly than as a serious candidate and, by his own admission, he hadn't a chance in a million of actually being elected.

"If I win I shall demand a recount," was the way he phrased it himself.

And of course you had supported Buckley with considerably less enthusiasm than you lavished on Goldwater, who came much closer to personifying the ideal of freewheeling libertarian individualism. Still and all, the election of John Lindsay, the candidate whom Buckley hoped to defeat by attracting Republican votes to his own Conservative Party candidacy, left you with a new sense of abandonment and homelessness, not unlike the state you were in following the Presidential campaign of 1960.

A new vacuum had been created. There was no figure in the

country who could qualify as a potential leader of a libertarian political movement with broad-based support. There was no political party or noteworthy organization, short of a few scattered discussion clubs, committed to the translation of libertarian principles into concrete political reality. The Republican Party was continually drifting further away from the quasi-libertarianism of the Old Republican Right Wing, and the Conservative Party of New York reflected for the most part the hard anti-Communist conservatism of William Buckley and *National Review.*

For this reason your attention was caught more and more by the ubiquitous Young Americans for Freedom. YAF was the largest and best-financed conservative group on American campuses, and though it was most heavily influenced by Buckley-style conservatism, there had been a vocal libertarian minority within its ranks since its founding in 1961. Your alternatives, so far as right-wing political activism was concerned, had been reduced to YAF–Conservative Party organizing or a kind of Ivory Tower purism which left you without any political affiliation at all. And so, in the early months of 1966, you found yourself at some rallies and conferences sponsored by YAF.

Attending a Young Americans for Freedom function in the mid-sixties was like entering a time capsule and being transported ten or fifteen years into the past. People looked exactly the way you remembered them half a generation before. In an age of long hair, jeans, and love beads, it was a mind-blowing experience to enter a convention hall in, say, the Waldorf-Astoria, and find yourself surrounded by a brigade of Pat Boones. The white bucks had been stored at the back of the closet by this time, but those freshly scrubbed cheeks and porcupine hairdos with needle spikes sticking out in six directions, the horn-rim glasses with translucent lower halves, the charcoal-gray slacks and red vests, the blue blazers with political-slogan buttons on their lapels were all over the place.

You immediately thought back to an age when the "other people," those degenerates in pegged pants, chartreuse shirts, and fuchsia socks were going at it hot and heavy with chains, bats, and homemade zip guns. You expected a battalion of them to invade at any moment, while Al Martino's "Here in My Heart" poured out of a jukebox in the corner—most urban neighborhoods had enjoyed at least one battle a week between Elvis Presley-style hipsters and charcoal-grayed Pat Boones.

Johnny Ray and Elvis and the Four Aces! Where the hell were they anyway? Where were Dion and the Belmonts and Buddy Holly and Ritchie Vallens and the Big Bopper and Sha-boom and Frankie Laine and the Four Lads and the Shirelles and Tab Hunter and Moondog and Al Hibbler and Don Cornell and Hamish Menzies and Anne Francis and Aldo Ray and the D.A. hairdo and the twelve-inch peg and Holden Caulfield and Grace Metalious and Debra Paget and Piper Laurie? Where were they all?

Why, they were right there in the Waldorf-Astoria, surrounding you at a YAF convention in the middle of the 1960's. And you loved every minute of it.

Until that inevitable day when you learned for the first time that there were people in the world who had never heard of James Dean.

James Dean! How could anybody never have heard of James Dean? Was there anything more important than James Dean in the 1950's? He was bigger than sputnik, bigger than the Russian invasion of Hungary, bigger than the English bombs raining on Cairo. James Dean was a revolution all by himself. He was even more important than Marlon Brando. He stamped a life style on an entire generation.

A whole generation of teen-age Americans walked around for years in red nylon jackets like the one he wore in *Rebel*

Without a Cause. Legions of red-blooded American high-school students with cigarettes hanging in the corners of their mouths were referring to their girl friends as "my friend," the way he'd introduced Natalie Wood to his parents. Legions more went on those school expeditions to the Planetarium and "mooed" out loud when Taurus the Bull came into focus on the ceiling.

James Dean was a way of life. James Dean was a teen-age rebel before anybody knew what the Establishment *was.*

And so you found yourself in the middle of a convention hall in the Waldorf, surrounded by people who looked like Pat Boone and made you think of people like James Dean and Johnny Ray—surrounded by people who *themselves* couldn't remember anything that happened before Peter, Paul, and Mary came along. More important than that, you felt a little sick with the understanding that if James Dean were to walk into the convention hall with his bright red jacket and his freaky lopsided grin, ninety per cent of the people there would consider him a Communist.

You knew now, suddenly and painfully, that this was not the way to Galt's Gulch after all.

With the first tremors of disillusionment, you started to take a closer look at the printing on some of those lapel buttons.

"Boycott Polish Hams!"

Why the hell would anyone in his right mind want to boycott Polish hams? Weren't we all supposed to be free traders? Didn't we all believe in the unregulated market place? What, in the furthest stretch of the imagination, did the Polish people have to do with Marx and Stalin? Were these poor bastards ensnared in a slave state by a tyrannical political regime to be further penalized by relatively free Americans who refused to buy their hams?

"Impeach Earl Warren!"

But Earl Warren could be good for you! We're individualists

after all, aren't we? Isn't Earl Warren making life easier for individuals who find themselves locking horns with a gigantic State apparatus? Do we want to give the State even more power to hound its hapless victims every time they sleep around with the wrong people?

"Stop Lenny Bruce!"

Oh no! Please no, not Lenny Bruce. Wasn't it Lenny Bruce who said communism was a drag, just like a great big telephone company? Didn't Lenny Bruce say capitalism gives people a choice, baby, and that's what it's all about? So what if he used words like "fuck," "shit," "piss," and "rape," and even "come." Didn't we believe in free speech? Didn't we believe that an individual should be allowed to do and say anything he pleased so long as he didn't hurt anyone else? And Lenny was funny, goddamnit! He was saying things that had to be said. So what if he made fun of nuns and priests and said they were screwing one another? If they weren't then, they are now. Who gives a damn anyway?

No, no. Not Lenny Bruce. Please don't kill Lenny Bruce!

It was through Young Americans for Freedom, whose founding in 1961 kept his right-wing coalition together, that Buckley exercised his greatest influence on campus intellectuals —those who would eventually take their place as speech writers, PR men, and other functionaries of the Republican Party. Buckleyite conservatives controlled most YAF chapters around the country, and with an adequate money supply and established organizational structure they were able to attract many Rightist students to the traditionalist position.

If Buckleyite conservatism characterized the great majority of the YAF membership, the second largest group, the libertarian faction, was most heavily influenced by Objectivism. Objectivism was the logical home for most young people with a libertarian bent—and, since the great majority of *Atlas*

Shrugged and *The Fountainhead*'s readers had never visited the seat of Objectivism in New York City, they had never come face to face with the Randian idiosyncrasies that inspired so many New York libertarians to make a more critical appraisal of Rand's ideas.

By the late 1960's sufficient friction had developed within YAF between the forces of William F. Buckley and those of Ayn Rand to cause frequent battles for control of various campus chapters. Since the YAF hierarchy was almost uniformly traditionalist, an attempt was made to purge Objectivists from leadership positions on the campus, which served only to escalate a situation of mutual distrust into one of downright hostility.

Looking back to the late fifties and the venomous assault *National Review* made on *Atlas Shrugged* in the form of a book review, it seems surprising that so many young Randians flocked to the YAF banner when it was raised in 1961. Rand herself had denounced Buckley and the New Conservatives as "immoral religionists," sharply criticizing those of her followers who had lent their "sanction" to the conservative movement. However, the shaky alliance between traditionalist conservatives and the Objectivists becomes less mystifying when you consider that Rand, for all her intellectual impact, did not have a political base of her own to offer young Objectivists. Many Objectivist students joined YAF for the simple reason that they had no place else to go in order to engage in political activities, and there is no question that most of them joined with the explicit intention of transforming YAF into an Objectivist-oriented political institution.

Though Randians and Buckleyites differed strongly on questions of religion, morality, and other key philosophical issues, they shared in common a rhetorical devotion to private property and a free-enterprise economic system. Tenuous though this bond was, it made it possible for YAF to become a political base of operation for young libertarians and young conservatives, forced by the absence of alternatives to share one in common.

According to the results of a poll conducted by the leadership of YAF and released in January, 1970 in the *New Guard,* twenty-two per cent of YAF members considered themselves libertarian, naming Ayn Rand and Ludwig von Mises as their chief sources of influence.

Seventy-two per cent cited William Buckley, Russell Kirk, and Frank Meyer as their intellectual leaders, and of this number nine per cent were Frank Meyer "fusionists" who stood somewhere between the libertarians and the traditionalists.

The remaining six per cent were "radical traditionalists," who might also be regarded as fervent American nationalists. The intellectual pillars of this faction were Buckley's brother-in-law, L. Brent Bozell, a fanatical convert to Catholicism who later founded the Sons of Thunder, a neo-Carlist paramilitary organization whose members, wearing red berets and rosary beads, invaded hospitals to baptize aborted fetuses; Henry Paolucci, an ardent American nationalist; Robert Welch, founder of the John Birch Society; and explicitly anti-Semitic followers of Willis Carto, whose extremist right-wing combine came to include Liberty Lobby, the new *American Mercury* magazine, and another campus organization called the National Youth Alliance.

If one could draw a scale reflecting the spectrum of opinion within YAF—and within the right wing in general, since YAF can be viewed as a fairly accurate microcosm of the Right— ranging from radical libertarian on one end to radical traditionalist on the other, it would look something like the chart on page 60.

Anarchism

Ludwig von Mises Ayn Rand
22%
Libertarian

Frank Meyer
9%
Fusionist
or
Libertarian
Conservative

William F. Buckley Russell Kirk James Burnham
63%
Traditionalist Conservative

Henry Paolucci John Birch Society
L. Brent Bozell
6%
Radical
Traditionalist

Willis Carto
and
Right-Wing Totalitarianism

All these forces at work on the American Right since the early fifties had resulted in this rather shaky right-wing coalition. It was a combination of at least three elements: Buckley's appeal to the religious traditions of middle America, and his emergence as a "sophisticated" spokesman for the work ethic and the free-enterprise system; Rand and Goldwater's impact on young Americans with a penchant for radically individualistic alternatives to the American Corporate State; the creation of Young Americans for Freedom as a political base for the various types drawn to a libertarian-conservative frame of reference. A denouement of sorts was reached after the Goldwater campaign of 1964. The Right became disenchanted, to a large extent, with Goldwater's apolitical idealism and his "unrealistic" approach to power politics in the United States. Largely under the influence of Buckley, and later, Kevin Phillips who wrote *The Emerging Republican Majority,* the Right began to take a more "pragmatic" and less doctrinaire course over the next few years.

The logical end to this trend was, of course, the candidacy of that most pragmatic and fence-straddling political hack of all, Richard Nixon, in the Presidential campaign of 1968.

The Right Wing
Joan of Arc

Standing out there in the rain, distributing campaign leaflets.

"Nixon is the One!"

Oh Christ! Is this what it had come down to? This shifty-eyed con artist? You could tell by looking at his picture that he would never have been allowed near Galt's Gulch. He was tall enough, all right. And lean, though in a dumpy kind of way. But in your heart you knew he wasn't right.

Nixon wasn't the one, and everybody knew it. And yet you stood out there in the rain on the West Side of Manhattan distributing this pack of lies to anyone with his hand out. There was a certain percentage of people that would grab onto anything so long as it was free. And so all these liberals and wild-eyed West Side radicals would swarm on by, hatred spilling over their left-wing eyeballs, accepting their sheets of freebie propaganda even though they knew it reeked of fascism.

"Nixon is the One!"

This sleight-of-hand purveyor of shoddy goods from the

heartland of America? This all-American carny barker? You told each other he'd worked his way' through college selling worn-out French ticklers to pimply faced high-school boys. If Nixon was the one there was no hope for any of us. We might as well lock ourselves in the kitchen and turn on the gas jets. It was all over. It had all come down to this.

In your heart you knew Nixon wasn't the one, but in your heart you also knew that Hubert Humphrey was a freaked-out altruist on roller skates. Hubert Humphrey was a smiling kewpie doll. Hubert Humphrey was a left-over manservant from F.D.R.'s New Deal, a third-string water boy for J.F.K.'s Frontiersmen, who later choked on the table scraps from L.B.J.'s Great Military Society. Hubert Humphrey was a nebbish, a nothing, a nonentity.

Hubert Humphrey was Wesley Mouch.

What a hoax on the American public. After all the idealism, all the years of frustration, struggle, and disillusionment, the American political system had degenerated to this: a contest between the two most thoroughgoing political hacks either party could possibly have come up with. Nixon and Humphrey. Walking personifications of the worst elements of the two-party electoral system. The worst of the lot. The dregs. The built-in weakness of our representative democracy was out in the open for all to see. For all to see who wanted to see.

I joined the Conservative Club on the upper West Side of Manhattan thinking—naively, as it turned out—that the conservatives in this predominantly liberal area would tend to be more libertarian than they were, for example, in the Throgs Neck section of the Bronx with its heavy concentration of Birchers. And so I attended the weekly meetings expecting to join forces with local libertarians who, however obnoxious most of them might be personally, would at least be motivated by intellectual rather than prejudicial considerations. What I found instead, piling out of the ornate, thick-walled town houses along Riverside Drive and West End Avenue, was a collection of bejeweled dowagers and monocled relics who tended to claim blood relationship with virtually every crowned head of nineteenth-century Europe.

Then there were the older West Siders who remembered their area when it was predominantly Irish, with a scattering of German and Italian families. They were mainly low-income Law-and-Order types who had never achieved the wherewithal to move up to Riverdale or into the suburbs, and they resented bitterly the heavy infiltration of blacks, Puerto Ricans, Haitians, Dominican Republicans, Cuban refugees and struggling artists, actors, and writers who had all but taken over the neighborhood by the early 1960's. Since I counted myself as a member of the last group, I had a difficult time adjusting to their notion of how a conservative society should be organized.

At the first few meetings I was somewhat startled to see several club members sporting George Wallace buttons on their lapels and dresses, but I dismissed them as a small, fringe element. The official policy of the club was to support Nixon, and except for a few pre-convention posters calling for the nomination of Ronald Reagan, the slogans on the walls and the campaign literature were strictly Nixon. But as the campaign progressed, the percentage of Wallace supporters grew in size and volubility, until by the early fall, Wallace campaign posters were appearing alongside the Nixon posters. When I first protested to the club leader, he told me not to worry.

"They're only a handful of kooks."

Later on he admitted that he couldn't be sure until he walked into the voting booth which way his vote would go, for Nixon or for Wallace. Nixon simply was not "strong enough," and was too much of an opportunist to be trusted.

The high point of each weekly gathering usually occurred in the final minutes before adjournment. It was provided by an incredibly ancient woman, so old in appearance she could have been anything from a dissipated seventy-five to a well-preserved one hundred and six. She was invariably groomed to the teeth, covered from head to foot with shining beads and baubles and gleaming silken gowns from an era long forgotten. She was referred to by everyone as "the Contessa"— assumed variously to be of Russian, Slavic, Lithuanian, or Serbian nationality. It is doubtful that anyone ever knew her name or her true geographical origin.

The Contessa would sit quietly through the evening's proceedings, through the reading of minutes and the various courses of action proposed for the following weeks. By the end of each meeting she would have had quite enough. With the assistance of her neighbor on either side she would rise, infirm of body if not of purpose, to her feet. Quivering with rage like an infuriated peacock trimmed with Christmas ornaments, she would raise a knotty little fist at the assemblage and cry out in brittle, rasping tones:

"You Americans are zo ztoopid! Zo weak, and nai-eef, and ztoopid wiz all your talk aboud elections. You must *seize* power, *seize* power, *seize* power. Before it is too late!"

But this would-be Joan of Arc, ready to charge the steps of the White House if only she could find a dozen red-blooded stalwarts, was delightful compared to the Bircher who came down a few weeks before the election from, as I recall it, the "Douglas MacArthur Chapter" somewhere in the Bronx. He was eager to inform us that he was all in favor of a democratic form of government under present circumstances. Of course, such indulgences as campaigns, elections, and Con-gressional checks on the President were necessary only up to the point when you finally established "the right kind of people in power." From that moment onward competitive elections would serve only to waste the taxpayers' money and create a climate of confusion. America had apparently missed its golden opportunity when MacArthur failed to seize command after being recalled from Korea. Popular support for him had been "overwhelming," and a take-over by the beloved general would have been an expression of the "will of the people." Now, of course, the military was so heavily infiltrated with Communists one could not be completely sure that anything beneficial would result from a military coup.

What were you doing with these people anyway? For almost ten years you had managed to avoid the more exotic fringe groups on the Right, and here you were, in 1968, sitting in a political clubroom flanked by relics of a long-past age of aristocracy, and slightly deranged recruiters for the John Birch Society.

Ironically enough, the form of fanaticism adopted by the John Birch Society's founder, Robert Welch, had led him in the middle 1960's to adopt certain positions which bore a strange similarity to those being espoused by the New Left. He was fond of referring to the United States government as "our main enemy," and to the war in Vietnam as a "CIA plot" to destroy the military strength of the nation. The New Left had, of course, designated the United States as the "most imperialistic" country in the world, while denouncing the CIA —years before the Pentagon Papers—as the main instrument behind the assassination of Diem and the conduct of the war itself. One important difference in these two views is that

Welch saw the CIA as having been taken over by "agents of Moscow," while the New Left regarded it as a reflection of a deep-lying American sickness. Later in the 1960's, however, Welch began to join the traditionalist Buckleyite conservatives in their insistence on total victory in Vietnam.

It would seem that a simplistic view of world politics can have an appeal for the least intellectual elements on the Left as well as the Right. To those on the Right who find themselves totally mystified by the complexity of international affairs, Birchist theories offer a simple, easily grasped explanation for the continuing erosion of the American political system. How satisfying to blame it all on a "conspiracy"—the "Communist conspiracy," the "international Jewish-Communist conspiracy," the "world anti-American conspiracy"—it really doesn't matter what you call it. The more vague and preternatural the conspiracy is, the better. And the more mysterious and satanically powerful these international forces can be made to sound, the better it is for the advocates of the conspiratorial view. The last thing in the world they need is for the leaders of the conspiracy to be identified and brought to heel—they would then be forced to invent a new conspiracy to explain the evils afflicting American society.

Similarly, there are anti-intellectual forces on the radical Left who are equally hard pressed to understand the existence of poverty, hunger, oppression, exploitation, and privation in the world. Somehow, if these ills can be attributed to a single source the whole political process is brought down to a level even the most confused can understand. Enter the reverse side of the anti-Communist hysteria coin: America itself is inherently evil. The Enemy, for the unthinking Left, is *Amerika* with a K—K for Kill and Korruption. Right on, tiger! If only we can get that K out of Amerika, the peoples of the "Third World" will all be eating six meals a day. Just don't get too explicit about what that K really is. Don't de-

prive *them* of *their* conspiracy. K for racistfascistsexistKapital-
istimperialism is quite specific enough.

In the years right after college, from 1959 through the
middle 1960's, your affiliations on the Right had been limited
to those groups whose libertarian principles were adulterated
primarily by philosophical eccentricity or personal idiosyn-
cracies. The Randians and the Goldwaterites, whatever else
you could say about them, were motivated by a hunger for a
consistent, ethical individualism—which they could not translate into a viable political alternative.

Disillusioned with the hybrid libertarianism of Rand and
Goldwater as a means toward the desired end—a free society
—you had found yourself a fellow traveler on the traditionalist right of YAF and William F. Buckley, Jr. Leaving them,
you had somehow ended up supporting Richard Nixon and
consorting with ancient European ex-aristocrats and disciples
of a right-wing Society that even Buckley had denounced as
too authoritarian for his taste.

The facts were there, and had to be faced. Your continuing
Odyssey from faction to faction had only brought you further
and further away from the America you wanted to reach.

Around this time I met the Galambosian.

"I am a Galambosian," he said.

A *what?* I was beginning to feel like a right-wing Yossarian.
All these mothers were out to destroy every principle I believed in! If it wasn't square-jawed Southwesterners with mixed
premises, or Ivy League intellectuals who mouthed off in public
like truck drivers, or shifty-eyed carny barkers from the
Middlewest, it was an S. J. Perelman character with a pipe
and an ascot, telling me he was a Galambosian.

"What the hell is a Galambosian?"

There was this individual, it seems, named Joseph Andrew

Galambos who evolved a theory of "primary property rights." Apparently, as soon as someone came up with a new idea—whether an invention or an original philosophical concept—the prototype belonged irrevocably to him and was to be regarded forevermore as his primary property. Somewhere along the line Galambos picked up the notion that Thomas Paine had invented the word "liberty," whereupon he established the Thomas Paine Royalty Fund, and every time he gave a lecture and used the word "liberty" he dropped a nickel into his fund box as a royalty payment to Tom. How he determined that a nickel was the proper measure of homage to Mr. Paine, I have no idea. Legend even had it that Galambos was still diligently searching for Thomas Paine's descendants so he could turn over moneys due their famous ancestor.

Sometime in the early or middle 1960's, Galambos decided that his name, Joseph Andrew, was actually the primary property of his father. In order to avoid giving his father a royalty payment every time he spoke the name, Galambos reversed the order and sent out notices to all his friends that henceforth his name was Andrew Joseph, and that he was to be addressed as Andy, instead of Joe.

"There are five legitimate functions of government," said the Galambosian.

"No kidding. What are they?"

"I am not at liberty to say. The theory was originated by Andy Galambos and it is his primary property."

The Galambosian also informed me that Andy had been introduced to Ayn Rand several years before, and that after five minutes of conversation they had pronounced each other insane.

"Of course, it is Miss Rand who is really insane," said the Galambosian.

"Why is that?"

"I'm afraid I cannot tell you. The reasoning behind that theory belongs to Andy."

The most peculiar thing about the whole Galambosian concept was the impossibility of finding out anything about it. Galambos' disciples were not at liberty to disseminate his philosophy without paying a royalty to their leader—who could not even *waive* payment, since primary property was an absolute good and could not be given away. You were stuck with it whether you wanted it or not, throughout eternity. Consequently, all the converts were those proselytized by Galambos himself—a time-consuming and self-restricting process, it being physically impossible to convert more than a handful of people at a time.

"If the rest of us were free to discuss his ideas," said the Galambosian, "there is no question in my mind that Galambosianism would spread throughout the world like wildfire."

There was no question in my mind by the end of the 1968 campaign that a brain-spinning lunacy was spreading like wildfire throughout my own world. If I saw just one more "Support Your Local Police" or "Nuke the Reds" sticker, I knew I would lock myself inside my clothes closet and assume the fetal position.

I had seen enough protruding jaws, drilling eyes, and dollar-sign lapel pins to last a lifetime. There was only one proper response to anyone who firmed up his chin and talked to me of "second-handers" or international conspiracies—instantaneous violence. Whammo! Sock! Pow! Punch! Kick him where it hurts and then remove his tongue with a rusty fork. Rip off his "Bomb Hanoi" button and hammer it into his crazy skull. Draw and quarter the bastard and send the pieces to Ayn Barry Buckley Nixon Welch Galambos, Jr.

Sitting there in O'Neal's Saloon near Lincoln Center, staring through the picture window behind the bar at the great fountain across the street, you could get away from it for a while. Water jets shot in the air, fracturing into a billion parts, all on fire like gold coins under the still-bright November sun.

Ragnar Danneskjold! You were the only son of a bitch in the whole world who had a technique that worked. No more screwing around with slogans. No more shopping for compatible factions.

It's time to light up the sky with fireworks.

PART TWO
THE FRACTURE

7

A New Kind of
Telepathic Imperialism

GOLDWATER AIDE JOINS THE NEW LEFT!

That's what the headline said as I sat there in my 1967 Chevrolet reading the Mamaroneck *Times*. What the hell could you make of a thing like that?

I had left the city earlier in the day to hunt for a new apartment for my pregnant wife and young son. The further away from Galambosians and one-hundred-and-six-year-old right-wing Joan of Arcs, the better. Mamaroneck seemed as good a place as any. It was only forty minutes from Manhattan, right on Long Island Sound, and from the edge of town you could see the harbor where the boats with their white sails bobbed on the waves. Mamaroneck was as far removed from Upper West Side politicking in spirit as it was in miles, and still there was the headline in the local paper blazing as though it were written in fiery letters:

GOLDWATER AIDE JOINS THE NEW LEFT!

The sadists were following me!

Who *was* this one, anyway? Karl Hess, a former speech

writer for Barry. Most of his face was covered by a black beard, so you couldn't tell a goddamn thing about the bone structure. That was one strike against him right there. He obviously had something to hide. His eyes looked all right, clear and direct without a trace of shiftiness. Chalk one up for Hess. He was a little on the hefty side, and his muscle tone looked as though it could stand a lot of firming up. There was no question in my mind that he suffered from mixed premises and, probably, from some basic character deficiencies.

After working for the Republicans eight years or so, he was now calling himself an anarchist and a New Leftist. He was obviously trying to establish himself as a latter-day Ragnar Danneskjold, and I didn't like it one bit. Ragnar was mine, goddamnit, and I wasn't going to let his memory be dragged in the mud by a puffed-up ex-Republican who was ashamed to reveal the shape of his jaw.

On top of it all he had ruined a perfectly good day for me. It was impossible to concentrate on apartment hunting in Mamaroneck after coming across a thing like this. If I couldn't be left alone, if this Hess character insisted on hounding me like a driven rat, there was only one decent thing to do: stand up and fight back.

The career of Karl Hess as he evolved politically and philosophically through the 1960's has been fairly well documented in a number of articles published after his defection from conservatism in 1968.

Briefly, he was a major contributor to the Republican Party platform on which Richard Nixon ran in 1960. By 1964 he had emerged as Barry Goldwater's major speechwriter, and he accepted the number two post on the Republican National Committee prior to the Goldwater nomination in San Francisco. Like Goldwater, Hess was semi-anarchistic on domestic issues, advocating the strict curtailment of governmental power to matters exclusively concerning national defense. Again, like Goldwater, Hess had caught the paranoiac anti-Communist virus popularized in right-wing circles by Buckley and the *National Review* crowd in the middle 1950's.

As discussed earlier, the acceptance of dogmatic anti-communism by many on the Right divided the right wing into two broad camps: the libertarians who tended to be anarchistic on domestic issues and military noninterventionists in foreign policy, and the traditionalists who saw the existence of atheistic communism as a threat to the religious and cultural inheritance of the Western world. The most consistent libertarians, admittedly a small minority, rejected at the outset the notion that America had a moral obligation to maintain a strong military presence abroad to contain the spread of international communism; while the hard-line traditionalists supported Buckley's call for the temporary suspension of liberties at home until communism was defeated.

In the late fifties a third force developed on the Right in an attempt to bridge the gap between these two disparate factions. The "fusionist" school—as it was later referred to—found its spokesman in Frank S. Meyer, an ex-member of the Communist Party who had become an editor of *National Review*. Meyer maintained that it is possible both to keep our strong, militarized, outward-looking nation-state *and* to preserve fundamental individual freedoms in the domestic arena.

Many libertarians, finding Buckley's "temporary suspension" attitudes totally unpalatable, jumped for the philosophical life preserver Meyer had tossed out to them. Here was a way to eat their cake and have it simultaneously—to hang onto their libertarian rhetoric and keep their conservative credentials at the same time. Hess, Goldwater, and others somehow managed to gloss over the inconsistency of a small decentralized government that would be large enough to station nuclear-powered policemen in every potential hot spot in the world.

The schizophrenia inherent in the very concept of "libertarian conservatism" was bound to erupt in a major conflict sooner or later. The chasm was simply too wide for anyone to straddle comfortably over an extended period.

Hess, of course, threw off his anti-communism for total anarchism in 1968; Goldwater went the other way, forsaking much of his libertarianism for the traditionalism of Buckley, Nixon, and Agnew around the same time.

Following the Goldwater defeat in 1964, Hess wrote a book defending Goldwater's philosophy and the conduct of the campaign itself, thereby reaffirming his own dedication to the cause of fusionist conservatism. The book, *In A Cause That Will Triumph,* was published in 1967. It is likely, however, that he was already starting to question some of his own political and philosophical positions, notwithstanding the passionate rhetoric contained in his book. For one thing, conservatives had started to repudiate the elements of libertarianism remaining in Goldwater Republicanism, blaming the Senator's absolutist stand against the military draft and against every manner of social-welfare legislation for the landslide margin of his defeat. For another, Richard Nixon was resurfacing as the most likely candidate for the Republican presidential nomination in 1968, and Hess's estimation of Nixon, never lofty to begin with, had fallen substantially after Nixon's campaign in 1960.

And, finally, there was the issue of Vietnam. The horror of the war, combined with the conservative's demand for total victory at any cost, managed to get through to him. James Boyd quotes Hess on this matter in his excellent profile article in the December 6, 1970, issue of *The New York Times Magazine:*

> The immediate cause [of his defection] was Vietnam. Conservatives like me had spent our lives arguing against Federal power—with one exception. We trusted Washington with

enormous powers to fight global communism. We were wrong
—as Taft foresaw when he opposed NATO. We forgot our
old axiom that power always corrupts the possessor. Now we
have killed a million and a half helpless peasants in Vietnam,
just as impersonally as Stalin exterminated the kulaks, for
reasons of state interest, erroneous reasons so expendable
that the government never mentions them now and won't
defend them. Vietnam should remind all conservatives that
whenever you put your faith in big government for *any*
reason, sooner or later you wind up as an apologist for mass
murder.

If Vietnam was the major issue causing Hess to plant both
feet firmly on the libertarian side of the fence, the man most
responsible for getting him across it was Murray Rothbard.

Rothbard, along with Liggio, George Resch, and other libertarian purists, had maintained an independent presence on
the Right through the early years of the sixties. Rothbard en-
hanced his reputation as a leading Misesnian economist with
the publication of several books: a two-volume economic
treatise called *Man, Economy and State*; *The Panic of 1819*;
and *America's Great Depression*. He watched carefully when
Leonard Liggio established ties with several organizations on
the radical Left which, during this period, were growing more
active in their opposition to United States foreign policy. When
the Bertrand Russell War Crimes Tribunal was founded in
1966, Liggio assumed a prominent role; his disillusionment
with the evolving pattern of right-wing politics was leading him
more and more into the company of New Left groups like
SANE, SNCC, and SDS.

In 1965, Rothbard, Liggio, and Resch created Left and
Right, Inc., in New York City, and together brought out a
new journal which emphasized the common philosophical
bonds uniting the anarchism and isolationism of the Old Right,
and the instinctive pacifistic anarchism characterizing the New
Left in the middle sixties. Under the guidance of these two

Old Right libertarians, *Left and Right* was the first publication in the country to talk about a potential Left-Right political alliance, and it set the tone for the kind of articles on the subject which started appearing five years later in national magazines, from *Playboy, Penthouse,* and *Esquire* to *The Nation* and *The New York Times Magazine.*

But in 1965, the prospect of reaching a mass audience with these ideas seemed as remote as the most impossible of dreams.

The first important breakthrough for the concept of a Left-Right libertarian alliance came in June, 1968, when Rothbard published his article "Confessions" in *Ramparts,* the most widely read magazine on the radical Left. In it he set forth the Old Right position with its twin themes of domestic decentralization and nonintervention in foreign affairs, while pointing out the similarities between his own free-market libertarianism and the cry for neighborhood government and neo-isolationism that had already surfaced on the New Left. It was this article which caught the attention of Karl Hess, who by this time had begun to drift further away from the *National Review* Republicanism now dominating right-wing politics. Hess flirted briefly with Objectivism, and then he serendipitously discovered the *Ramparts* article.

In short, Rothbard reached him at the precise moment when he was most open to conversion.

Hess immediately called Rothbard in Manhattan, and for weeks they engaged in two-hour phone conversations, sometimes as frequently as two and three times a week, burning up the wires between Washington, D.C., and New York City with a veritable torrent of flaming anarchist rhetoric. When the time came for Bell Telephone to send its monthly greetings it became obvious that it would be far less expensive to carry on the dialogue vis-a-vis, so Hess journeyed northward to stay with the Rothbards on those quiet summer weekends when most middle-class New Yorkers are out of town, deepening their suntans on Fire Island and at the Hamptons. By the end of the summer the radicalization of Karl Hess had been accomplished. He was now a free-market radical, an individualist-anarchist in the tradition of Lysander Spooner, Max Stirner, Benjamin Tucker, Stephen P. Andrews, James J. Martin, Murray Rothbard, and Leonard Liggio.

An interesting footnote to this summer episode in the sweep of recent American history is the fact that while Hess was getting his head pumped full of anarchism by Rothbard and Liggio, he was also helping Barry Goldwater get re-elected to the Senate. When the campaign moved into high gear in September and October, Hess did most of the speech writing for Goldwater who was totally unaware of his principal aide's recent conversion.

It is amusing to thumb through some of the speeches the Senator made that fall and pick out the little seeds of radicalism Hess managed to plant. Consider, if you will, the spectacle of Barry Goldwater informing a conservative student body in the Southwest that he found some overlapping areas between his own philosophy and certain "anarchistic elements in S.D.S." When you note the number of times Goldwater referred to himself as "anarchistic" rather than the more acceptable (if only because more incomprehensible to the average voter) "libertarian," you begin to understand one of the fundamental weaknesses in the concept of representative democracy: most voters elect a candidate to a position of high power and authority for reasons other than the political issues involved, or the candidate's actual ideas. If John Lindsay were to go to Arizona and suggest that maybe some of the anarchists in S.D.S. aren't so bad after all, you would most likely be able to tabulate his vote with a counting glass. Put the same words in the mouth of Barry Goldwater, conservative Republican, and you're riding the homestretch with a winner. The consequences are not so far-reaching when local citizens vote their politicians into a position where they can control and regulate only the lives of their constituents, but it is a different story when a President or Congressman decides on questions literally involving the life and death of the entire country.

Hess's revitalized libertarianism of a decade before, its conservative embellishments neatly trimmed off by Rothbard and Liggio, grew within him throughout the fall of 1968. In December he called a press conference in his office in Washington, and announced that he was no longer a conservative, no longer a Goldwater Republican. He was an anarchist, and from this point on he would join hands with anarchist forces on the New Left with whom, he now discovered, he had more in common than he did with his former colleagues.

This was the story behind the headline that interrupted and then stopped my apartment hunting in peaceful Mamaroneck.

At the time I knew only that the decision had already been made for me: I would have to annihilate the bastard in print.

Look What Happened to Kerensky

My anti-Hess article was published in *The New Guard,* the official YAF magazine, in April, 1969. On the facing page, staring out defiantly at the reader, was Karl Hess's rebuttal, cleverly entitled "In Defense of Hess."

It was now apparent to me that this Hess fellow was the type of person who couldn't tolerate someone else getting in the last word under any circumstances. It wasn't enough that he had sent his message into Mamaroneck that day in December and upset me so much I was forced to head back immediately to Manhattan. Or that he had followed this assault with an article in the March, 1969, issue of *Playboy,* which I discovered on my way to its centerfold and O'Neal's one afternoon. No, his lust for power was so complete he had even followed me into the pages of *The New Guard.* Where, just a short time before, Galambosianism had threatened to relieve me of my last vestige of sanity, now a form of left-wing Goldwaterism loomed on my horizon as the most formidable challenge I had yet faced. As much as I longed for a life of tranquillity, I had no choice but to gird myself for all-out combat.

When Hess and I were asked by YAF to debate at a convention in New York City's Hotel Commodore, I looked forward to this opportunity to demolish him at close range. A week or so later, I received a copy of the flyer advertising the convention and discovered that what I had been led to believe would be a face to face clash with Anarchist Hess had now been scheduled as a four-way panel discussion among, besides Hess and myself, Frank S. Meyer of *National Review* and Professor Henry Paolucci, lately of St. John's University, whom I remembered as a fervent nationalist given to wearing socks that never matched when he taught at Iona College ten years before. The YAFers, exercising their overkill mentality as they are wont to do, had apparently intended to stage a three-to-one gang up on Hess. Having originally lined up Paolucci and Meyer to work him over, they'd decided as an afterthought to include me for additional security.

By the time I entered the convention hall for our so-called "debate," I had decided not to play the game.

I was introduced to Frank Meyer and Henry Paolucci before we went up to the rostrum. Meyer seemed preoccupied, but Paolucci immediately launched a twenty-minute monologue on his idea of the real hero of the Russian revolution, Kerensky, whose demise only proved that the Right could never establish political alliances with the Left no matter how much their immediate goals coincided. When I asked him why we shouldn't support the New Left on specific issues such as the anti-draft movement—since so many conservatives, theoretically at least, were also opposed to conscription—he rose on the balls of his feet and fairly screamed over the din in the hall:

"Look at Kerensky! Look what happened to Kerensky!"

Paolucci called himself a "libertarian nationalist," a grotesque contradiction in terms if there ever was one. He had a mystical reverence for the American nation-state, attributing to it those divine characteristics which most people reserve for their religious institutions. How he ever reconciled an ethic of individual freedom with the concept of an elitist collective order intrinsically superior to all other collectives on earth was a mystery to me then, and remains so, despite the fact that I have heard him elaborate on the subject on several occasions. He managed to blend St. Augustine, Plato, Thomas Aquinas, Adam Smith, and Mussolini in an eclectic grab bag philosophy which defied reason—or, at least, *my* reason.

With it all, he had his own private following among young conservative students, and there are still upper-echelon YAFers who refer to themselves as "libertarian nationalists" with a look in their eyes that is an open challenge to argue with them on the topic. There are the uncompromising defenders of the regimes in Formosa, Spain, Portugal, Greece, Rhodesia, and South Africa; and they will look you full in the face and tell you there is more freedom in these countries than you will find anywhere in the world except, of course, in the United States.

At the time the panel discussion was to begin, Karl Hess had not yet arrived. The three of us took our places on the podium, and moderator Arnold Steinberg, a libertarian-conservative who was then editor of *The New Guard,* decided to start without him. As Steinberg got set to introduce us to the audience, Hess, bearded and casually dressed, entered the rear of the hall with a long-haired hippie entourage—Rothbard's group of free-market anarchists, as I later learned. Rothbard moved down the aisle through their midst, in his undeviating attire of rumpled suit, key chain draped from the belt, white shirt, and bow tie reminiscent of the bobby-sox era.

Here was an irony contained within an irony. Into the vortex of this vast sea of conservative, middle-class youth swirled a small school of bearded radicals whose love beads swung from their necks; at their center stood their leader, more middle class in appearance than the most conservative YAFer in the house. Rothbard's reputation as a Mencken-esque, bumptious, curmudgeonly theoretician had preceded him, but the image was immediately dispelled.

Hess, on the other hand, had moved sartorially as well as politically to the Left. He looked a nicely balanced mixture of General U.S. Grant and Fidel Castro as he strode to the podium, his knotty black curls bunched behind his ears, a frizzy coal-black beard covering most of his face. He seemed outgoing and friendly as he shook hands all around. The basic amenities finally over, Steinberg called for order and got the meeting under way.

Frank Meyer was the first to speak. He gave a fifteen-minute presentation, criticizing Hess indirectly by condemning "unprincipled alliances" with the Left. It was his position that conservatives could never join forces with the New Left— even on such issues as the military draft which he, too, opposed in principle—because the motivation of the radical Left was actually to weaken the U.S. military presence in Vietnam. Meyer would have preferred to see the Communists wiped out by a "voluntary" and "professional" strike force, but since it was mandatory that we win in Vietnam, conservatives must take care to separate their anti-draft sentiments from their position on the war. In other words, the draft should be re-pealed eventually, but not until the war was won. When he finished his address he announced that he was already late for an appointment and would have to skip the question period. This caused considerable consternation in the audience; the odds against Hess were suddenly reduced to two to one.

Hess then rose to deliver a low-key, conversational synopsis of the position he had set forth in his *Playboy* article. It was inconsistent to preach individual liberty and local government out of one side of the mouth while calling for a vast, centralized military complex through the other. Anybody really against conscription should give more than just lip service to the anti-draft movement. The New Left was doing something about it while the Right just talked. Motivation wasn't important; top priority should be given to the attainment of a common goal regardless of one's reasons for desiring it. Again, conservatives talked a lot about decentralized power and neighborhood schools when the subject of busing came up, but they had reversed their positions rather dramatically when the black communities of Harlem and Bedford-Stuyvesant wanted the same policies for their own schools. In summation, Hess was urging the Right to become more radical and more consistent in its opposition to centralized power in Washington, and to re-evaluate its stand on military victory in Vietnam, which he considered immoral as well as strategically disastrous.

The immediate reaction to all this was a smoldering quietude emanating from the great majority of the audience. Rothbard and his anarchists did their best to take up the slack with applause and cheering, but it was evident that their demonstration was strictly localized. From the rostrum you could hear a few cries of "Get the Commies out of here!," "They don't belong here!," and "Send them back to S.D.S.!"

Now it was my turn, and I rose to speak with a clear idea of exactly what had to be done. Obviously, both factions were drifting further and further apart into extremist positions. It was up to me to present a well-balanced alternative, blending the best elements of conservatism and anarchism, enticing everyone back to the sane and solid center. Each extreme had become blinded by the light of its own dogma. If they could all just remain open to the voice of reason and sanity, there was every hope that moderation might win the day, and a final breach be avoided.

I spent the first few minutes talking about Hess's "wishful thinking" in expecting the Communist military threat to disappear simply because we didn't want to fight any longer. I said that anarchism could work only in a world in which everyone agreed not to try to conquer his neighbor by force. The crowd was warming to this theme and beginning to respond audibly when I suddenly shifted to the domestic area.

The federal monolith was now bureaucratized and rigidified to a degree that would have been unrecognizable twenty-five years before. Conservatives had been adamantly opposed to the expansion of the state-corporate system for more than forty years and it was extremely inconsistent, now that they were in the White House, to become such zealous defenders of the *status quo*. Conservatism was meaningless if it merely involved taking over a structure passed on by state socialists and somehow "trying to make it operate more efficiently." Working exclusively within the system was not sufficient to bring about the kind of changes that were called for. I was against violence, but nonviolent resistance to coercive state and state-supported institutions was justifiable on the grounds of simple self-defense.

I then catalogued a program of civil disobedience advocating, among other things, active resistance to the military draft; refusal to pay taxes; boycott of the public school system in those areas where it was centrally controlled, and the creation of storefront schools in the neighborhoods as an alternative; establishment of community police patrols to replace such municipal armies as "New York's Finest"; local control of streets and thoroughfares to regulate the flow of traffic and, consequently, automobile pollution; and neighborhood seizure of property that had been abandoned or condemned by the city for so-called "urban renewal."

The response was not at all what I expected. I had hoped that my dual message of qualified anti-communism and radical opposition to the impersonal corporate state would strike a responsive chord in just about everyone present. Not so. Hess, Rothbard and company, anticipating a crowd-pleasing denunciation of their position, were elated; YAFers tended to respond either with inaudible hand clapping or outraged hostility. One young fellow, who stood on his chair to denounce me for failing to recognize the "Red menace" sweeping the nation's campuses (I couldn't be completely sure whether he was referring to Maoists or American Indians), was treated to a two-minute standing ovation.

More perplexed than anyone else was Henry Paolucci, bobbing up and down in his chair, turning red, obviously itching for the chance to get in his licks. Apparently, with the unexpected disappearance of Frank Meyer, the three-to-one gang up on Hess had suddenly become, in Paolucci's mind, a two-to-one assault on the "libertarian nationalist" from St. John's.

He fairly pounced on the microphone and, fists waving, sailed immediately into an anti-anarchist tirade. Arnold Steinberg attempted to readjust the microphone downward a foot or so to accommodate the speaker's height; Paolucci, trembling with evangelical fire, refused to relinquish his grip and continued his address. He had grown up in an anarchist household, he maintained, and had experienced firsthand the tyrannical fist of an anarchistic *patria potestas.* He had heard enough talk of "this brand of gradualistic anarchism" in his life to know that it was nothing more than a subtle form of subversion, a device to lower the guard of the nation while treasonous forces corroded it from within. All the beauty, wisdom, and truth of Western civilization had reached apotheosis with the American nation-state, and it was the foremost duty of every loyal American to defend this heritage against the onslaught of barbarian and heretical alien forces. Individual freedom could be permitted only within the framework of an orderly preservation of the American religious and cultural tradition. (Buckleyites in the audience nodded their heads, perhaps recalling their leader's denunciation of those who reject contemporary American values as "excommunicants" who automatically forfeit their right to freedom.)

Somewhere along the line Paolucci also condemned the "tyranny of voluntary association," which was somewhat unnerving since conservatives had always invoked the *freedom* of voluntary association as their reason for opposing neighborhood integration.

He finished to a thundering ovation: the YAFers, to a man, rose and demonstrated their appreciation for a solid three minutes. This was the stuff they had come to hear. They wanted no wrist-slapping critiques of Hess's "naïveté": no wishy-washy speculations on the "impracticality" of anarchism. They wanted the body of the traitor strung on high for everyone to see, and Paolucci was stringing it.

During the question period Mario Rizzo, a Fordham economics major and a member of the Rothbard contingent, rose to his feet. Having acknowledged his willingness to accept questions from the "rabble in the corner," Paolucci listened patiently: Why, Rizzo wanted to know, shouldn't those who did not subscribe to traditional American values be allowed their freedom so long as they remained nonaggressive in their behavior toward those who did?

Now, Mario Rizzo at this time was a smallish, rather swarthy young man with dark, coarse hair and a long hooked nose. Paolucci sized him up for at least ten seconds and then finally replied:

"You! You of all people should be the last to criticize the concept of freedom within a stable religious order. Your people have been nomads for centuries, rejected by every society you ever lived under. Now your people have found a home, a home offering an opportunity to live in peace and freedom for the first time in history, and all this country asks in return is that you respect its traditions and express a little gratitude once in a while. . . ."

Mario Rizzo stood there, stunned by this unexpected revelation of his family's nomadic past. For twenty years he had been living under the delusion that his grandparents had come straight over from Naples without being rejected by anyone along the way.

It took a few minutes longer for him to take in the situation: there he was, a self-respecting Italian-American from Queens, unaccountably being Jew-baited by a pro.

I left the convention later in the afternoon secure in the knowledge that Henry Paolucci was the most evil man who walked the earth. Looking back, I doubt it. My only regret, when I remember that day in April, 1969, is my oversight in failing to check Paolucci's ankles. To this day I still don't know whether his socks were matching or not.

A Claque of
Porcine Revolutionaries

My situation at this point had boiled down to this: after nearly a decade of contact with virtually every conceivable right-wing faction, from Objectivists to Birchers, I was now imbedded in the midst of all of them *at the same time.* Whereas before I could size up each faction individually and at close range before traveling on to the next, I was now caught in a maelstrom of ideological furies representing every conceivable point along the starboard political spectrum.

So far as the immediate future was concerned, I could retain my affiliation with the Right and attempt to libertarianize the conservative alliance from within; I could join forces with the right-wing anarchists and try to build a viable movement independent of all others; or I could drop out entirely and find some peace of mind away from any form of ideological or physiognomical coercion.

I could eliminate this final alternative at the outset. In an age of electronic surveillance and telepathic authoritarianism, the earth had been reduced, in effect, to a global village. There was no patch of green, no valley, no glade, no grove of trees, no Gulch—I was sure of it now—that lay beyond the reach of space-age imperialists. Choice number three was out of the question.

So was choice one—libertarianizing the conservative Right. Elementary principles of self-defense, notably a concern for the preservation of my mental stability, required that I be removed as far as possible from square-jawed religionists, Ivy League Hegelians, Catch-22 Galambosians, or Paoluccian nationalists. The debilitating influence of ideological osmosis was far greater than I had ever realized.

That left choice two: embracing free-market anarchism and turning it into a realistic alternative to traditional liberalism and conservatism on the Right, and to rampaging adventurism on the Left. That meant making libertarianism the voice of the sane and moderate center.

The responsible anarchist center, so to speak.

This would also afford me the opportunity to keep a close eye on Karl Hess, who was apparently determined to follow me through the news media no matter where I went. By aligning myself with him and his associates I could at least protect myself against the unnerving prospect of opening up a newspaper or magazine in my most private moments and finding his hirsute visage. It would also give me a chance to rein in his compulsive gallop toward extremist positions—indeed, to lend a moderating influence to the whole anarchist movement while it was still in the process of development.

Several days after the convention at the Hotel Commodore I received a phone call from Walter Block, a disciple of Rothbard's. He invited me to join him and a few friends at his apartment on the upper West Side near Columbia University. My first reaction on walking into this den of anarchists was to decide immediately that there was no hope for a *détente*. Somehow, the spectacle of a half-dozen or so pudgy radicals sitting around on a Saturday afternoon, lapping up incredible mounds of ice cream and cake and talking anarchism and resistance, was not what I had anticipated. A barroom full of inebriated wire lathers taking time out from a football game on television could have wiped them out in a single encounter. This overweight crew would be lucky to find itself swabbing the deck on any ship of Ragnar's.

However demoralized by the sight of them, I had to admit as I listened that in theory, at least, this was my kind of stuff. Revolutionary capitalism. Uncompromising individualism. Free-market radicalism. Jeffersonian democracy revved up with a supercharge. State authority broken down to the minus n^{th} power—decentralization all the way to the level of the individual. The prospects were intoxicating. Their program was nothing less than the culmination, the absolute and final *logical reduction* of everything I had ever believed in.

I couldn't turn away at this point: Hess would never leave me alone anyway. These puffy, myopic revolutionaries had possibilities. With the proper kind of work—and exercise— they just might be transformed into a battalion of Ragnar Danneskjolds. They were raw clay ready to be molded and hammered into shape. The potential was fantastic—we could build a movement that would rock the nation.

How in Christ's name could anybody turn his back on an opportunity like that?

Once I had decided to jump into the anarchist arena on the Right, the next step was to assess the prospects of creating a viable Left-Right political coalition. Under the broad umbrella of anarchism, the libertarian fringes of both sides ought theoretically to be able to join hands in an anti-state radical movement. Both the radical Left and the libertarian Right were opposed to the war; both favored the massive reduction of America's international military presence and a return to military neo-isolationism; both endorsed the concept of a volunteer army to replace the military draft; both opposed our state-corporate economic system and central planning by a ruling elite in Washington; both favored political decentralization and the control of essential institutions at the local level.

Where the New Left and libertarian Right differed primarily was in basic economic theory. The Left spoke the language of socialism and communism with a small "c." They talked a great deal about the "people" and a system of "humanitarian socialism" in which "people" would control the facilities of housing, education, police and fire protection, sanitation, health, and welfare in their own neighborhoods. The right-wing libertarians were committed to the rhetoric of *laissez faire* capitalism, free trade and open markets. Their decentralist theories went further than the New Left's; they spoke of "Freedom to the Individual" rather than "Power to the People." But the greatest obstacle by far to the realization of a Left-and-Right libertarian alliance was the issue of private property. Right-wing anarchists were ardent private propertarians, maintaining that there could be no real freedom for anyone outside a system of self-ownership and concomitant protection of the right to own land and other property; the radical Left, for the most part, still clung to the Marxist and anarcho-communist dictum that "property is theft."

Still, as serious as these divisions were, in actual practice there might not be so much difference between a system of decentralized neighborhood "socialism" and individualistic free market "capitalism." Both concepts reflected ideal positions, and the best either side could hope to achieve in the near future was a modified version of both. At the worst, if free-market radicals and neighborhood socialists did wind up locking horns over thorny issues like private versus community ownership, their battles would at least take place on a smaller scale than Washington, D.C.—or City Hall, for that matter.

Instead of, say, disputes involving eight million New Yorkers representing six dozen private-interest groups, there would be thirty or forty thousand, and five or ten private-interest groups. Weren't small problems theoretically more manageable than large problems? There would be less bureaucracy involved, less chance for power brokers and grafting administrators to hide inside a jungle of red tape. Fraud, graft, and corruption would be more visible to everyone, and the neighborhood Hitlers would be easier to lay hands on than the ones in City Hall or in the White House.

It was not utopian and not panacean. It was far from perfect, but perfection was impossible when you were dealing with imperfect people. So long as some people insisted on attacking or cheating their neighbors, there would be a certain amount of violence and fraud in the world. Until the millennium arrived and everyone was a practicing libertarian, there would be people all over the place engaging in nonlibertarian activities. All right, you'd have to have police protection and courts of arbitration. But the idea was to break down the power and break down the problems into smaller units. To diminish the measure of political power while increasing the measure of freedom and self-ownership for every individual. To keep the ideal in mind, so we'd at least be heading toward it instead of away from it, hoping to get as close with each step as was possible within the limits of human imperfection.

Even the most poverty-stricken neighborhood would be better off in a decentralized system. Take, for example, Harlem and Bedford-Stuyvesant in New York City—certainly among the poorest in the nation. We know that betting on numbers there is a billion-dollar-a-year enterprise. *A billion dollars a year in spare change spent on a daily numbers lottery in poor black neighborhoods!* At present, however, this activity is declared illegal by City Hall which has, in effect, granted a monopoly on numbers running to racketeers who pay the police to look the other way. The billion-a-year is now siphoned out of the community into the already affluent neighborhoods of Bay Ridge in Brooklyn or Country Club in the Bronx.

Why shouldn't this money be permitted to remain where it is needed? Why shouldn't all gambling be legal (it is a non-aggressive activity engaged in by consenting adults), and the numbers lottery be run by local groups with an interest in improving their own neighborhoods? It is not true that poor areas do not have the wherewithal to solve their own problems. They are prevented from doing so by centralized authority which stifles local initiative and acts to grant monopolistic power to well-financed lobby groups such as those of oil, steel, the defense industry, and the Mafia. Anybody should be able to see that all of them, working hand in hand with the politicians, are what "organized crime" is all about.

My first exposure to any groups on the radical Left took place during a meeting at Columbia University. Several of us had gone there to hear Leonard Liggio and Ralph Schoenman, former assistant to Bertrand Russell, lead a discussion on the American presence in Vietnam. Left-wing groups of every description were swarming in, lining the walls after the last seats were occupied. They tended to cluster according to their affiliation, as did the groups on the Right. There were Wobblies with "IWW" buttons on their blue-denimed chests; YAWF-ers (Youth Against War and Fascism), many displaying "Al Fatah" buttons on their shirts or fatigue caps; Maoists; left-wing and right-wing Trotskyites; right-wing Marxists who favored the Soviet invasion of Czechoslovakia; and anarcho-Bakuninites who supported the Czechoslovakian rebels. The factionalization on the Left was, if anything, even more pronounced than that of the Right, and I remember thinking that Nixon need not lose any sleep if this was his opposition.

"These people are crazy," someone remarked to Walter Block when we had taken our seats.

"Of course they are," he said. "But right-wing crazies are crazier than left-wing crazies."

Maybe so, but I wasn't really prepared for this. My first inclination was to turn around and head back to more familiar terrain. After all these years of experience, I had at least grown accustomed to the vagaries of the right-wing mentality. This ideological jungle on the Left seemed impenetrable.

Ralph Schoenman began his talk, then went on to talk and talk some more until some members of the audience were calling for him to shut up. He went right on, pouring out an unpunctuated verbal cascade that seemingly had no ending. After a full hour of this ranting monologue, voices were being lifted from every section of the hall. One man in his middle fifties—dressed in steel-tipped boots and generally resembling the archetypical proletarian hero on a 1920's Communist Party wall poster—rose to his feet and raised his fist.

"I'm a worker!" he identified himself. "What are you? You're nothing but a goddamn bourgeois armchair socialist who never worked a day in his life!"

This sparked heated outcries from other factions in the room. A woman, fortyish and rather shopworn, as though too many years of inner turmoil had taken their toll on her once-pretty features, was the next to speak. She identified herself as a member of the Communist Party and then proceeded to excoriate Schoenman for suggesting that the Soviet Union was guilty of anti-Semitism. According to her, the Communist State in Russia was a paradise of racial and ethnic tranquillity. As proof she cited the fact that some obscure Jewish journal was still being published, unmolested, after more than forty-five years.

Next it was the Wobblies' turn. A young man in his thirties, built like a dockworker, his shirt sleeves rolled up to expose his forearms bulging with huge knots of muscle, got up and called everybody in the hall "a bunch of fucking fascists!" Apparently all of us except the Wobbly and his group had deviated years ago from the true Marxist-Leninist line. We were all "revisionists," if not "running dogs of fascist imperialism." Just when it appeared that he was about to throw himself on the nearest fascist, he unaccountably sat down and began to sob quietly. The moderator took this opportunity to praise the assemblage for their "democratic spirit" in allowing everyone to have his say. It was only at a socialist conference that one could find such a spontaneous outpouring of sentiment, and unsquelched sentiment at that.

"Socialism means peace or it means nothing at all!" was the way he wrapped it up.

By this time the crowd was too wound up to listen much longer and Liggio was forced to limit his remarks to a synopsis of what he wanted to get across. The infighting among the various groups continued on a more subdued level, but it threatened to break out of control at any moment. Liggio concluded quickly and the meeting was adjourned.

Reeling out of the hall later in the night, I found my sensibilities under attack once again. You don't leave the realm of right-wing eccentricity just to get yourself entangled in the corresponding area on the Left. The path to truth and sanity was obviously strewn with obstacles at every turn. You had to step gingerly and watch your footing, or you'd lose your balance at any moment.

The moderate anarchist center, now discovered, could be obliterated from both sides.

10

Deviationism
Rides Again

It was during this period that the Radical Libertarian Alliance was formed.

In addition to Walter Block and Karl Hess, Murray Rothbard had gathered around himself quite a group of followers in the New York area. Most of them, college students and recent graduates, had been converted to libertarianism through the writings of Rothbard, Rand, Mises, and other libertarian authors. The concept of a Left-Right libertarian coalition had been Rothbard's dream from the early years of the 1960's, and he had been trying to involve right-wing anarchists in the anti-war movement as early as 1965.

The Rothbard circle had remained small and manageable throughout the 1960's, but the defection of Karl Hess and the ensuing publicity he received, particularly on the Right, attracted a good many more right wingers to the anarchist position.

By the late spring of 1969 Rothbard's apartment could no longer accommodate his followers, and so monthly dinners were arranged in certain West Side restaurants. To give these gatherings a semblance of structural formality, an organization was proclaimed and given a name: the Radical Libertarian Alliance. Hess and Rothbard decided that a publication would accelerate the proselytizing of further converts from the conservative Right, and under their joint editorship the *Libertarian Forum* appeared shortly after as the official RLA publication.

The first dinner attracted nearly a hundred people from New York City, New Jersey, and Connecticut. The libertarian "movement" had moved out of a living room and into the public arena.

The next logical step was to take the offensive.

We had to blitz the opposition before it could recover from the "debate" at the Commodore. YAF, as the most visible and symbolic conservative group on campus, was our most likely target. We would perform a surgical operation on the YAF overbody and slice off the left wing—the twenty-two to thirty-one per cent ranging from moderate to radical libertarian. Almost everybody to the right of Meyer, and certainly to the right of William F. Buckley, could be dismissed at the outset. We could expect our highest scores among the Randians, Misesnians, and the more libertarian of the Frank Meyer fusionists.

This was my kind of stuff. This was ballsy. The time for screwing around was finally over. It was time to get out in the ring and slug it out. No rules, no holds or punches barred. Whammo! Sock! Double him over, get him on his knees and kick him in the eardrum.

Nonviolently, of course.

Blitz, then rip away. We had our own paper organization now. The Radical Libertarian Alliance. We had a home for disaffiliated YAFers to turn to. They would need a way station when the rip-off was over, a place to get their wounds licked and their heads straightened out. A bed to recuperate in before going out on their own to establish local RLA chapters.

All we needed was some cadre and we were off. A national political movement. Rip off, succor, build. That was the combination. A nation-wide Alliance, Ragnar-ready to knock the military-industrial-political complex on its ass. It was beautiful. It was even possible. If only it didn't bomb in New Haven. The *new* New Right. Climbing in bed with the *old* New Left, the disorganized and disillusioned New Left that was falling down on its back a little bit more every day. Didn't disheartened New Leftists need a home just as much as split-off Rightist libertarians?

We set our sights on the YAF national convention in St. Louis, Labor Day weekend, 1969. Buckley would be there. So would Al Capp. And Barry Goldwater, Jr., sporting a jaw like an upside-down anvil, a jaw that put even his father's to shame. And Buzz Lukens and Fulton Lewis and a whole array of right-wing luminaries—politicians, journalists, columnists, intellectuals, an entire gallery of sitting ducks lined up on the same podium. Hess was flying in from Washington, and I was going with some RLA people from New York.

It was shaping up to be one hell of a time.

And so it came to pass as planned.

Of a total of twelve hundred delegates attending the convention, a full three hundred and fifty were separated before the third day was over. The key wedge driven between the libertarian and conservative forces was, of course, the military draft. The conservatives had sponsored a resolution calling for a volunteer army to replace conscription. In opposition to this, the libertarians submitted a list of minority planks demanding immediate withdrawal from Southeast Asia, a repudiation of domestic oppression as well as the Communist variety, legalization of marijuana, and *active resistance* to the draft.

The conservatives, predictably, were opposed to any measures which side-stepped legal channels. As libertarian planks were defeated one by one, the demoralization in libertarian circles became more and more evident. When it was obvious that the radical anti-draft resolution would also be hammered to extinction, the final polarization was achieved, and in the most dramatic manner possible—a draft-card burning incident.

The spectre of a young rebel standing in the midst of a right-wing political rally, a burning card lifted over his head, was a truly breathtaking sight to behold. It was equivalent to reading an excerpt from *Radical Chic* at a Black Panther fund-raising dinner; to singing the praises of a guaranteed annual income in Ayn Rand's living room; to calling the pope a Mafioso at a meeting of the Italian-American Civil Rights League.

At that moment the impending libertarian-conservative schism on the Right escalated from ideology to invective and, finally, to physical confrontation. After a few confused moments of punching and shoving and general commotion, the division was complete. There could be no turning back.

The libertarian conservatives had been radicalized, and in something like ten minutes.

They stalked out. They held their own caucus. They agreed to form a separate organization—the Society for Individual Liberty, as it was later named—independent of YAF and all other conservative groups. This new organization's founders, Don Ernsberger and Jarret Wollstein, further agreed to join RLA and other libertarian clubs in creating campus chapters for the express purpose of splitting away as many libertarians as they possibly could from the conservative right-wing alliance.

They said, "thanks but no thanks" to William F. Buckley and his conservatives—thanks for defending us from "heresy" all these years, but now we'd like to find some way of defending ourselves from our defenders—if it's all the same to you, old boy.

At first it appeared that we had taken on more than we could possibly assimilate.

This libertarian herd suddenly inherited by RLA comprised a multifaceted assortment worthy of inclusion in anybody's gallery of American oddities. Most were Objectivists, whose leaders included a Randian super-hero with a penchant for showing up all decked out in a black stretch suit with an enormous gold dollar sign embroidered on his chest and a gold lamé belt cinching his waist. Someone ventured to remark that all he needed to complete the image of a freaked-out capitalistic superman was a gold cape swirling from his shoulders—and he was immediately informed that the cape did indeed exist, but was kept for at-home wear lest its owner call undue attention to himself in public.

Then there were the Randian "heads," most of whom belonged to free-market anarchist organizations located in Southern California. I wondered if there wasn't something in the water of this region that transforms everyone who migrates there into a bizarre distortion of his former self. Here were devotees of Ayn Rand, disciplined to the restraints of Objectivist logic when in their native habitats, who emigrated to L.A. and points south and immediately began to blow their brains on acid, and turn in their business suits for beads, jeans, and shoulder-length hair while they talked about the "groovy," "outasight," "wild and funky" market place. Capitalists to the sixteenth power—joining communes, trading one another for cigarettes, pencils, candy, food, and pot in their own self-contained economic system—they were outwardly indistinguishable from the Jerry Rubin/Abbie Hoffman communal anarchists of the New Left.

There were the right-wing dropouts, retreatists who wanted to secede from the United States altogether and build an ocean platform, a seaborne Galt's Gulch beyond government jurisdiction where they could establish their own free and uncontrolled trading community. Others, who called themselves trogs, wanted to burrow under the earth and create an underground city—"Sink City," no less—undetected and undeterred by the restrictions of authoritarian political regimes. Some of these envisioned having their own atomic bomb for defense purposes, along with a private space program so they could homestead portions of the moon in the name of liberty "before the fascists gobble it up."

There was an Objectivist Homophile League for young males who were more turned on by John Galt than they were by Dagney Taggart, or for *femmes* who dug Dagney more than John. There were radical entrepreneurs who wanted to remake the United States into a gigantic shopping center owned and managed by a single real estate concern, thereby eliminating the functions of the United States government; libertarian royalists who thought wealthy individualists should buy up large tracts of land and turn them into fiefdoms under a libertarian code of justice; anarcho-Minute Men who wanted to take to the mountains a la Che Guevara and organize a revolutionary guerrilla movement for intransigent free enterprisers; radical reformists who favored moving all the libertarians in the country into a single state, Nevada or Wyoming perhaps, and taking over the political structure through the elective process.*

Some were disciples of Robert LeFevre, a self-styled edu-

* This concept was actually attempted on a limited scale by some members of the Gay Liberation Front to establish their own community, and other radical groups from all over the political spectrum are entertaining the possibility for themselves.

cator in California who refers to himself as an Autarchist. He coined this title, translating literally as "self-rule," to distinguish himself from the anarchist tradition dominated by collectivists such as Proudhon, Bakunin, Kropotkin, and the anarcho-syndicalists of the nineteenth and early twentieth centuries. LeFevre is a raw individualist whose enterprises include a private school called Rampart College and a quarterly magazine through which he disseminates his credo of uncompromising capitalism. LeFevre is equally contemptuous of liberals, conservatives, socialists, communists, and collectivists of the anarchist school with whom, unlike other free-market anarchists, he sees no hope for an eventual Left-Right coalition.

Autarchists are also called radical private propertarians, since they maintain that an individual is entitled to all the land he can see from any given point. This was bad enough when people were limited to mountain peaks with a visibility of thirty or forty miles, but in an age of space travel it is conceivable that a particularly self-centered individualist might orbit the earth and claim the whole ball as his personal domain. Presumably, according to the Autarchist code of ethics, this space-age landlord (earthlord?) would then have the right to charge his three and a half-billion tenants rent under the threat of being shuttled off into unclaimed space. One can envision a society in which the poorest tenants are confined to the cheaper plots in Antarctica, while land in the temperate regions is rented at a premium to the wealthy.

Still others were advocates of the philosophy of Max Stirner, a nineteenth-century individualist. Stirner, who has been described as Ayn Rand in a bad mood, promoted a kind of rampaging individualism that makes Nietzsche look like a Germanic version of Wesley Mouch. He recognized no moral code whatsoever, and, in fact, considered any talk of moral restraints on human behavior to be an intolerable abridgment of individual liberty.

And so the list went, on and on, boggling the most stable and well-fortified of imaginations. As likable and human as many of these students might seem when compared to the spectre of an army of Objectivist slaves marching in orderly precision to the beat of Randian drums, they were hardly the stuff to offer as a viable political alternative to the most dictatorial of political regimes.

"What are we going to do with these motherlovers, these morons, these cretins?" Professor Murray Rothbard was practically vibrating in his armchair, his bow tie on an angle.

"To know them is to hate them," offered Walter Block.

"They're deviationist creeps!" Rothbard continued.

Oh no! Not again. I heard enough of that crap when I was an Objectivist. I didn't deviate from conservatism to start denouncing other people for deviationism!

"Not deviationism," I said lamely.

"The right-wing deviationists are walking around with their goddamn dollar signs plastered all over the goddamn place, and the left-wing deviationists are destroying what's left of their brains with acid and pot."

Let them. Let them do anything they want to so long as they don't hurt anybody else. Let's not start the bullshit all over again. There's room for everybody who's nonaggressive, who's nonviolent: the weak, the insane, the lame, the strong; those with square jaws and receding jaws, with no jaws at all— even those with two jaws; those with dollar signs on their foreheads and gold-plated pricks; and those who blow their minds on acid six times a day.

"We're too small to start worrying about deviationists," said Block.

"We aim for quality, not quantity." Rothbard's mind was made up. "We can't accept all the shit that walks in off the streets."

There it was, but there *we* were. Now that we had fractured the right-wing alliance there was room for everybody in the responsible anarchist center. We were in the process of building a home, a resting place, an organization big enough to squeeze in everybody in the whole goddamn world if only they agreed not to hurt each other.

The sane and moderate anarchist center was already under attack, it seemed, more from within than from either the Left or the Right.

PART THREE
THE COALITION

Greed Is What Makes the World Go Round

Columbus Day Weekend, 1969: a libertarian convention, the first of its kind, was sponsored by the Radical Libertarian Alliance. Now that we had all these homeless right-wing radicals on our hands, we had to give them a place to rest their heads. If we waited too long a sense of alienation might set in and drive them back to the motherly arms of Bill Buckley or the fatherly caress of Ayn Rand.

We couldn't waste a moment. We had to move while everyone was still in a state of shock, still trying to figure out exactly what had happened. The RLA convention at the Hotel Diplomat in New York City, coming barely a month after the YAF affair in St. Louis, would serve as a rallying point for our homeless legions. There we could begin the process of molding them into good libertarian radicals, unyielding free-market rebels. A battalion of Ragnars charging en masse against the state. A hundred thousand revolutionary individualists tearing away at the American eagle feather by feather, claw by claw. Christ Almighty! It was so beautiful I couldn't stand to think about it.

"We'll get the right-wing and left-wing deviationists in the same room and chop off the fringes. We'll drive them miles apart."

"Not *apart,* Murray! *Together,* for Christ's sake. We'll weld the fringes into a solid anarchist center. A moderate and responsible libertarian middle. Leave the polarization to Nixon and Agnew."

A giant Left-Right libertarian coalition: left-wing anarchists and acid-dropping love children; middle-class tax resisters and blue-collar hardhats; right-wing free traders and intransigent individualists. We had to make them know each other and respect each other. Love, maybe even understanding, was too much to hope for. So long as they respected one another and agreed to leave everybody else alone. That was the ticket. Anything else was doomed to failure.

They hitchhiked in from Canada, they bummed rides from the West Coast, they drove up in Morgan Plus-Fours and new Chryslers from Florida and the Deep South.

We had business executives from the Midwest whose vest pockets bulged with bank accounts and credit cards. We had twenty-year-old Objectivists from campuses all over the country. We had love children, real live love children with beads and sleeping bags and a serene gentility glazing their eyes. We had some giggling teenyboppers from Washington, D.C., and at least two matrons from Atlanta, Georgia. We had communal anarchists from Pennsylvania and Maryland who devoted all their time to arts and crafts, and hard-eyed profit mavens from Minnesota who got horny reading *The Wall Street Journal.* We had three hundred of the most unlikely and most diverse types imaginable who had traveled clear across the continent to learn how anarcho-communists and private enterprisers could live together harmoniously in a libertarian society.

That was the idea, anyway.

The first sign that things might not proceed exactly accord-

ing to plan occurred about a half-hour before the opening
address. People were filing in, buying their tickets at the door
and fastening name cards on their shirts and jackets—an orderly procedure all around. People who hadn't seen one
another in six months or a year were shaking hands and
getting re-acquainted; others were being introduced to
strangers. Everyone was smiling and talking pleasantly, long
hair and jeans chatting with stiff collars and business suits.
A truly happy opening.

Until, suddenly, a voice rang out:

"Mary's destroying the coalition!"

Who? What? What the hell was going on? We hadn't even
gotten *started* yet! Don't let anybody wreck the coalition before it even gets off the ground.

People were running out into the corridor. Necks were cran-
ing as everyone rose on his toes to get a better look at what
was going on. For Christ's sake, it was true. The coalition was
in jeopardy. Mary, the dirty rotten bitch, was beating the shit
out of a love child!

Mary was all the worst aspects of women's liberation rolled
up into a hundred and eighty pounds of flaming terror. Mary
wasn't big, she was gross. She had a pair of shoulders on her
that made Jimmy Brown look like a ninety-pound weakling.
She had thick black hair that stuck out fourteen inches in
all directions. If she stared too long at you with those fiery red
eyes you could feel your nuts roasting between your thighs.
She was Ayn Rand on a two-week binge. She was a super-
heroine shot through with sixteen hundred volts of electricity.

To complete the image, she had dressed herself all in black.
Her wide shoulders and broad-beamed back were covered with
a shiny jet black shirt, and she wore an arm band with a
clenched red fist along her biceps. She had on a pair of tight
black jeans that revealed every contour of her muscular
thighs, her black calf-high boots were polished to a mirror

shine, as were the dollar-sign brooches that adorned her collar tabs on both sides. I was willing to concede that she might even qualify as a "right-wing deviationist," although I had come to despise the term.

There was Mary, over in the corridor with this emaciated love child from Pennsylvania, slamming him back and forth against the wall and screaming at him.

It seemed this dreamy-eyed communalist had been regaling some Objectivists with stories about his "extended family" in Pennsylvania, telling them how it was out there in the country-side, away from all the factories and automobile exhaust. Everybody loved everybody, and they all spent their days making sandals and weaving straw into backing for rocking chairs. They swam together in the raw in a pond behind the farmhouse, and wrote poetry in the evening before climbing onto a big mat on the floor and fondling one another. They had loved being off in the woods by themselves, away from technology and civilization and greedy profiteers.

Greedy profiteers! Mary's eyes lit up and hatred shot out of her eyes the way sparks do from a toy machine gun. This anti-life collectivist was attacking greed? "Profiteers?" This puny little altruist was badmouthing the *profit system?* Mary could contain herself no longer. It was at that point that she stepped forward and grabbed the anti-mind second-hander by his bony shoulders and started to slam him back and forth against the wall.

"Greed! Greed! Greed's what makes the world go 'round, you degenerate altruist son of a bitch, you filthy little whim worshiper, you collectivist creep!" she screamed over and over while she punished his body again and again.

Somebody knock her down and sit on her, goddamnit! Tape her mouth with Band-Aids and throw her out in the street! Damn it all, she's destroying the coalition! Don't let her get away with it!

"Quality, not quantity. We have to skim off the cream and throw out all the rest."

"Consolidation, Murray. There's room for everyone in the moderate center."

Maybe the retreatists had the right idea after all. Drop out. Get away from it all. Build your platform out in the ocean and run your own system the way you like. Dig into the ground or stake out a cave and find happiness in Sink City. Away from all the nonsense, away from all the bullshit. Maybe lunar homesteading was the only real alternative after everything else was said and done.

Now an apparition in olive-green battle fatigues materialized in the corridor, surrounded by a personal entourage of sartorial imitators.

What the hell's going on this time around? Necks crane once again as people swarm to greet the olive-green apparition. Who the hell is it now?

"It's him. He's arrived," a voice called out.

"Who's arrived?"

"The Field Marshal of the Revolution."

The what? The bloody what? Has the whole world gone insane? The Field Marshal of—I looked, then choked before I could get it out.

For Christ's sake, Karl. Give us a break, will you? You can't mean it. Say you're not serious, will you for God's sake? There he was, the funkiest looking revolutionary in fifty states, with a wardrobe fresh off the rack of Abercrombie & Fitch. Combat boots laced to the top with rawhide strips; olive-drab pants cinched in at the waist with the biggest, knobbiest, most outasight belt buckle you ever saw in your life; khaki shirt opened to the third button so his chest hairs stuck out; sheepskin hunting jacket to ward off the October chill; and, *pièce de résistance,* a green Fidel Castro fatigue cap with a black and red Wobbly button pinned over the peak. All in all, an easy two hundred clams' worth of proletarian garb.

Karl, you crazy son of a bitch, say you don't mean it! Oh, but he's not even smiling.

The college kids from Fordham, Rutgers, and points west were flipped out, goggle-eyed, and you knew, you just *knew* that before the week was over they would scrape together every dime they could lay their hands on and get themselves a revolutionary outfit just like it.

The matrons from Georgia and business executives from Kansas just stood around self-consciously, shifting from foot to foot. Was this the same, was this really the same gentleman who used to write speeches for Barry Goldwater? One could not be quite sure with all that facial hair and those knotty curls that stuck out like grapes underneath his cap.

The olive-green satellites stood to the side, smiling, talking about their "outasight" trip up from Washington. They had all ridden in the back of Karl's jeep, they said.

Jeep?

Yes, of course. It had to be a jeep. A dark-brown or olive-green one, no doubt.

You didn't expect them to drive up like that in a brand new Cadillac, did you?

"Lop off the fringes and keep a good purist libertarian center. We can't accept any deviationists and we don't need any crazies. Let everybody else keep the crazies. We'll build a good, solid, *quality* movement."

You can't lop off the fringes, Murray. You can't drive the crazies away because *everybody* is crazy. If we polarize all the deviationists, there won't be anybody left in the goddamn center!

There were banners on the wall to please every faction

imaginable. On the wall behind the podium was an enormous black one with red letters: POWER TO THE PEOPLE!

That was a grabber for the Left.

Slightly to the right of it was an equally large black banner with gold lettering: LAISSEZ FAIRE! A natural turn-on for the profit mavens in the crowd.

To the right of this, just as large and just as prominent, was the final banner: SOCK IT TO THE STATE!

This one was for everybody, Left, Right and in between, since they were all radically opposed to the liberal-conservative *status quo*. We had all the props, all the psychological ploys and P.R. bait laid out like a spider web. This was the rallying point. We had built our rest home, our way station, in the Hotel Diplomat, right in the middle of Times Square.

Joe Peden was calling for order. Everybody take their seats. The conference is about to begin. Rothbard, Liggio, and I were on our way to the podium when I saw him.

I saw *him!*

It was the Galambosian. He had followed me from the upper West Side of Manhattan all the way down to West Forty-third Street. He was probably right behind me that day in Mamaroneck for all I knew. He was looking at me now, he was smiling at me. He *recognized* me.

"I am now an anarcho-Galambosian," he said, shaking my hand.

Leave me alone, I don't want to hear about it. Now I know why Lenin needed his Cheka. That's what we need now more than anything else, a libertarian Cheka. A secret police to take care of all the goddamn deviationists.

"The anarcho part of my philosophy is my own primary property. I'd be glad to discuss my modifications to Andy's system whenever you have the time."

Never! I don't care about it, I don't want to hear your modifications now or at any time in the future. Just leave me alone before I start lopping off the fringes right this minute!

"Sure," I said. "I'll be glad to hear about it later, when the first panel discussion is over."

From the podium you could get a good overview of the crowd.

The business executives and the Southern matrons were huddled together front and center, fidgeting nervously in their seats after having witnessed the pre-convention activities in the corridor. Mary and her anarcho-objectivists were just behind them, unfurling their black flags embellished with red fists and gold dollar signs. The hippies, long hair matted under sweaty Indian head bands, blue-denim shirts limp and soiled after several weeks of wear, sat across the aisle from Mary and her friends, understandably wary.

The leader of the Objectivist forces in St. Louis was in the balcony, where he had set up a table to advertise his organization and offer paperback copies of Rand's novels and other right-wing literature at a discount. Although he was wearing brown slacks and a glittering sharkskin suit, I expected him at any moment to disappear inside a phone booth and resurface in black leotards, predictably emblazoned. He was not yet twenty-five years old, but there was no question in my mind that he would have a novelty store in Times Square offering black-and-gold whips to sex deviates by the time he was thirty.

The olive-green revolutionaries, the Field Marshal situated in their midst, were at the opposite end of the balcony casting sour glances toward the sharkskinned profiteer and his display table. Between them, and scattered randomly throughout the orchestra seats below was a sampling of quieter libertarian types, including the lone Galambosian. All of a sudden the Galambosian was beginning to look like a purist middle-of-the-roader.

When the discussion finally began and the first condemnations of the state-corporate system echoed through the hall, a horrifying roar rose from the audience. Mary and her troop were on their feet, black flags waving wildly over their heads, right fists lifted straight up in the air.

"Strike! Strike! Strike! Strike!" their voices rang in a loud, paralyzing chant, sending shivers down the spines of the industrialists in front of them, and an ominous chill throughout the entire audience.

One could only sit back in awe, wondering what kind of hellish fanaticism had suddenly been released at this conference which was supposed to be devoted to the principles of justice and individual liberty. The whole world *had* gone berserk.

That night it was Hess's turn. The Field Marshal of the Revolution poured forth a message to match his attire. Strike! Assault! Direct action against the state!

How could you keep up with a guy like this? His swing from the Goldwater Right to the Left was breaking the ideological sound barrier. The matrons and business executives were riveted to their chairs, too dumbfounded to move. Mary and her friends were beside themselves with ecstasy, on their feet once again, waving their flags and fists.

"Strike! Strike! Strike! Strike!"

"Which side of the barricades will you be on when the chips are down?" Hess asked hard-eyed from the podium, menacing the profit mavens and other right-wing libertarians in the audience. He had perfected a way of asking questions so that they sounded like threats. "There is no neutral ground in a revolution," Hess continued in his best CAUSE THAT WILL TRIUMPH manner. "You're either on one side of the barricade or the other," he said, cleverly paraphrasing Eldridge Cleaver's

"You're either part of the problem or part of the solution" ultimatum.

At that precise moment the polarization was complete. Mary and her friends were joined by the love children, left-wing anarchists and adventurists, and other cultural New Leftists, all of whom were on their feet shrieking!

"To the barricades! Shoulder to shoulder with our brothers and sisters of the revolution! To Fort Dix tomorrow morning!" This last representing a spontaneous collective decision by the Leftists to join the war-protest march on Fort Dix the following day.

The other half of the crowd remained in its seats. The division was clean down the middle. The right-wing anarchists, moderate Objectivists, and business types sat in stone-faced opposition to the radicals singing and chanting maniacally around them. The emotional release was almost sexual. The revolution was here and now, you could feel it all around you. Tension! Violence! Instant action! At that moment, there was no question in the minds of the radicals that the government would be in ruins by tomorrow afternoon and that they would be occupying the seats of power. All were caught up in the intoxicating delusion of collective invulnerability. Troops? Tear gas? Bayonets? With a determination and solidarity of purpose such as this, how could anything stop them?

Sunday morning the conference reopened to an audience of fifty. The Leftists were all off in the wilds of New Jersey, singing and chanting as they marched on Fort Dix. Most of the right-wing libertarians, including the Midwestern industrialists and the garden-variety Objectivists, had gone home in disgust. Out of an original crowd of over three hundred, that left fifty "centrists" who were determined to hold their ground and salvage what they could of a splintered movement that never really got started in the first place. The fringes were lopped off, the corners rounded—although in a way not anticipated. The deviationists had been driven off in different directions to parts unknown. We were left with fifty middle-of-the-road anarchists.

Informal speeches and panel discussions continued into the middle of the afternoon. Along about three o'clock, while somebody was droning on about nonviolent resistance and constructive alternatives, the quiet of the hall was interrupted by a loud commotion in the corridor. Fifty heads whipped around to the rear, one hundred ears strained to hear what was going on. A loud bellow in the corridor and then a crash as the doors swung open.

It was Mary, of course. Standing at the rear of the hall, a vision straight from the flaming depths of hell. Her black shirt and arm band were in tatters. Her feet, her bare dirty feet— where the hell are your boots, Mary?—were planted squarely on the floor in the manner of a slugger ready to trade you blow for blow.

Finally she started her slow approach down the center aisle toward the rostrum, her shoulders and arms swaying heavily with a power all their own, her eyes shooting hatred in all directions as she moved. Now she reached the front of the hall and mounted the podium steps, her heavy bare feet slapping loudly against the wood.

"WHERE THE FUCK WERE YOU?" her voice, amplified through the speaker system, zapped the hall.

"DO YOU KNOW WHAT IT'S LIKE TO BE TEAR-GASSED?"

No threats, Mary. Just tell us what happened, please.

The Fort Dix demonstration, it seemed, had got out of hand. Instead of marching in orderly fashion along the prescribed route to protest the war, the demonstrators had formed an assault force and gone charging toward the stockade where some G.I. dissenters were being held.

"DO YOU KNOW WHAT GAS DOES TO YOUR EYES? DO YOU KNOW WHAT IT'S LIKE TO FEEL YOUR GUTS ON FIRE AND YOUR LUNGS CLAMPED IN A VISE?"

We're sorry it happened, Mary. But you must have known they would retaliate before you did it. What did you expect from them anyway? Those soldiers out there, all dressed up in helmets and fatigues, all just as frightened as you are, all trapped in the system just like anybody else.

"WHERE THE FUCK WERE YOU?"

And then it was all over. She caved in on herself and fell over like a rag doll. Jets of salty tears issued forth from the fiery coals, and rivulets ran down her cheeks onto her lapel pins.

Don't cry, Mary, we'll get the ones responsible for it one of these days. But you don't fight atom bombs with knives and sticks, Mary. David and Goliath was a fluke. Nixon, Agnew, and L.B.J. and all the rest of them are the enemy, not some bunch of weekend soldiers who'd rather be anywhere else, doing anything else but guarding a military base on a Sunday afternoon. We'll get the real enemy, Mary! But not with knives or rocks or stones. That's *their* way. That's what they're hoping for. Nothing drives the middle class into the arms of the administration faster than violence, and the politicians know it better than anybody else. There's a better way than that. A radical and revolutionary way, but a nonviolent way.

Do you understand, Mary? Nonviolent revolution is the only way to get back at them.

Now the rest of the Fort Dix contingent was storming back into the Hotel Diplomat. Back to the center. Back to their home.

"Hurry!" they were yelling. "We have to get out of here, the place will be alive with feds and fuzz in no time flat! They're after us, they're after Hess. They're after everybody." Rumors spun around the hall, a new one every second.

The first libertarian conference was now over.

Ragnar Lets Me Down

12

It was a beautiful day in the middle of fall, 1969. How long had it been since I last set foot on the Fordham campus in the northeast corner of the Bronx? Ten years? Fifteen years? Oh my God, could it possibly have been *fifteen years* since I strolled across the Quadrangle in white bucks, red corduroy jacket, shirt and tie, and the spikiest crew haircut you ever laid eyes on? Now I was back again, though in a new role: to address a group of Fordham anarchists.

It was an eerie feeling, walking the concrete walks past Hughes Hall half a generation later. The gray stone buildings wrapped in vine, the neat rectangles of lush green grass were exactly as I remembered them.

As was the huge field across from Hughes Hall. I remembered the way it used to be: every spring they'd erected a giant statue of the Virgin Mary in a corner of the field and smothered it with tons of flowers. May was the month of Mary, and every day after lunch the entire student body of Fordham Prep would be compelled to mass out in the field

127

for a community rosary service. Fifty-five or sixty hapless freshmen were drafted to represent the Hail Marys and Our Fathers in the five decades of the rosary, which meant forming a chain of human rosary beads around the statue of the Virgin and leading each prayer when your turn came. It was usual for the token Negro accepted at Fordham each year to be appointed the Apostles' Creed—he had to stand apart from all the others, a black island alone in a sea of white and pink. Intended as an honor, this designation no doubt served only to remind the Apostles' Creed of his ethnic uniqueness at a time when he wanted more than anything else to blend inconspicuously into his surroundings.

> *Mary, Mother of Our Master,*
> *Just a Statue Made of Plaster!*

Several hundred pink-and-white faces with sports jackets, shirts and ties; one black thumb in the midst of them all nervously reciting the Apostles' Creed.

> *Jesus, Jesus,*
> *Come and Squeeze Us!*

The field of grass was cut to a quarter-inch to match the haircuts of the students.

> *Mary, Mary, Dressed in White,*
> *Will I Go to Hell Tonight?*
> *Mary, Mary, Dressed in Blue,*
> *I'm a Pig, I Love to Screw.*

For a few minutes there you're sixteen years old in the early Eisenhower years, the years when the most exciting campus demonstrations were the weekly football or basketball rallies. Of course, you strained your throat screaming Rah! Rah! and Go! Go!, and maybe even blackened someone's eye at the inevitable beer bash that took place in a neighborhood saloon after the game—at sixteen you were already learning to guzzle with the best of them.

But the illusion of recaptured youth lasts only as long as it takes you to make a closer examination of your environment. The grass and trees and gray stone buildings cloaked in ivy are still the same, all right. But not the people swarming by —these students are different, these students don't belong here. Oh my God, Fordham's campus has been invaded by legions of heretics and nihilists. They chased the white bucks and crew haircuts off the premises and filled it with blue jeans and long hair. And black people, too. Not just a token Negro or two from Pelham Bay or Jackson Heights. But a battalion of wild-eyed militants with electrified Afros and variegated dashikis. That's okay for Berkeley or Columbia. But *Fordham?* It's subversive.

It's also ruining my nostalgia.

But who're you kidding, anyway? White bucks? Charcoal grays? Johnny Ray? All in the past. There's a war going on now, and these kids are its victims. Innocent lives are being destroyed and you've already decided to take your stand with the innocent. You grew up in an age when the National Guardsmen on campus were there to recruit new members, not shoot down students. Nobody who grew up in an age of peace has any right to resent the presence of the victims on his campus.

So a renegade from the Pat Boone era, himself now stepping along in denims and boots and granny glasses and a mustache where last he trod in white bucks and a needle-spike hairdo, returned to the campus of his youth to spread the message of anarchism and resistance. You see him moving by, an ex-conservative and ex-writer of articles for right-wing journals of opinion, hurrying along a concrete walk where once he ran on his way to class, to address a gathering of students who want to know the best way to overthrow the government of the United States. The same government he swore he would defend when he joined the Marines at twenty years of age;

the same government he thought was the freest in the world when he blackened someone's eye at a beer bust back in 1955.

But all that was so terribly long ago, so very, very long ago. For a minute it had seemed like yesterday, when you saw the trees and grass and ivy-covered gray stone buildings. For one long second you *felt* sixteen again.

But it was really so terribly long ago after all. My, my, how the times have changed. All that was before the war; all that was before the riots; all that was before the napalm and the bombs; all that was before they shot Fred Hampton and Mark Clark at four o'clock in the morning; all that was before they killed the kids at Kent State and Jackson State; all that was before they murdered James Rector at People's Park; all that was before My Lai and Song My; all that was before the Bay of Pigs and the Gulf of Tonkin; all that was before the Conspiracy-to-Commit-a-Conspiracy trial in Chicago; all that was before surveillance and dictatorship by dossier; all that was so terribly long ago.

You knew now that your government wasn't the freest in the world after all. You knew now that your government was a bloodthirsty tyrant, an anachronistic claque of imperialistic lunatics who could kill civilians with abandon today, and listen to Billy Graham talk about Jesus Christ the following morning in the White House.

You knew now that whatever the cost, your government would definitely have to be stopped.

Just as I anticipated, the Fordham contingent had fitted itself out with revolutionary outfits to the last man. Many wore olive-green and khaki, carbon copies of Hess at the October convention right down to their Wobbly buttons. Others opted for blue jeans with dark blue T-shirts under light blue work shirts open at the collar. And most of the clothes were crisp and spanking new, still smelling of camphor from the neighborhood Army and Navy store.

These were my Ragnars, my revolutionary individualists, separated now from YAF and ready for combat. Legions of libertarian radicals straining at the bit, itching for the chance to lay their hands on Nixon, Johnson, and a few others, and trade them to Hanoi for American POWs.

It was going to be so easy. Organize! Strike! and bring him down! One, two, three, and it's all over. Swift and surgical. A minimum of bloodshed—you just emasculate Goliath and drop his carcass in the middle of the Atlantic. There was no doubt in anyone's mind that by the beginning of the summer of 1970 at the very latest, the government of the United States would be out of the catbird seat never, never to return again.

But wait! Something was wrong. All was not going according to script. I listened, not sure I could believe what I was hearing.

"Comrade———has the floor now. As you all know, Comrade———has been working with the Student Progressive Labor Party to unionize the workers in the cafeteria. He. . . ."

"Comrade———has been busy these past few weeks building a bridgehead with representatives of the Socialist Workers Party. We're planning to join them in their Campus Radical Front to keep local merchants from purchasing California grapes. . . ."

"Comrade———has been organizing neighborhood welfare workers to set up picket lines around. . . ."

Enough! Have you all gone mad? We're supposed to be building *strategic* alliances with the Left, not turning ourselves into a bunch of goddamn Marxists. We're trying to create a Left-Right *tactical* coalition and convert the Marxists to libertarianism, not the other way around. You've all become a bunch of crazy left-wing deviationists!

Mind you, these were the same students who had traveled out to the YAF convention in St. Louis, filling the chartered buses with their short-haired, horn-rimmed glassed, regimental-tied, drip-dry suited and oxblood-broganed bodies while they shouted things like "Nuke the Reds," "Bomb Hanoi," and "Impeach Earl Warren." Now, three months later, they sat around a conference table at Fordham University in prole shirts and combat boots, calling each other "Comrade" and talking about their "brothers and sisters" in the Maoist-oriented Progressive Labor Party. Instead of "Nuking the Reds" they now wanted to "Off the Pigs," neatly transferring their fanaticism from one object of hatred to another.

"Comrade————is organizing a group of brothers and sisters to hold open the doors of subway cars during morning rush hour and distribute leaflets to exploited workers."

Clever. That one will really go over big. Some poor bastard who's going to be docked an hour's pay because he's ten minutes late is really going to be radicalized by that tactic. Sure you'll get converts that way. You'll get a kick in the nuts and a punch in the teeth, that's what you'll get.

"I really believe in doing my own thing," said Comrade ————. "The only problem is, when I feel like doing my own thing nobody will do it with me."

That's the point of doing your own thing in the first place, dumbnuts. If everybody did the same thing, it wouldn't be *your* thing anymore, it would be everyone's thing.

It was clear to me that the moderate anarchist center was being blitzed from all sides. Apparently, everybody in the whole world had become a deviationist.

Were these my *free-market individualists* sitting around a conference table in prole garb and calling one another Comrade?

Ragnar, you son of a bitch, you let me down again!

13

I Fail to Make
a Citizen's Arrest

After Fordham, we decided to launch major assaults on both our flanks. There was no question that we were beginning to get a bit paranoid about our developing "movement." For the first time since I could remember, libertarianism had a decent chance to become something more than an intellectual pastime, and we had become a little hypersensitive about having our prospects destroyed by our extremist fringe elements. There was only one proper thing to do at this point: we had to thin our ranks.

Rothbard kicked it off in the November 15, 1969 issue of the *Libertarian Forum* with a flaming attack on ultra-Left adventurism. While the Left was reeling with the aftereffects of the first blow and the Right was feeling comfortable in its own brand of heresy, I drove in the first shaft on our starboard flank with a blistering swipe at the Objectivists. Rothbard followed with a second blast at anarcho-communism, indirectly criticizing Karl Hess whose swing to the Left was still accelerating at a breathtaking rate.

133

Now that we had the left- and right-wing deviationists on the ropes, I cold-conked our right-wing libertarians with an attack on lingering conservatism in their ranks. In March, 1970 Rothbard annihilated the entire New Left with a headline article entitled "New Left, Rest in Peace," which was followed by another piece called "Farewell to the Left" and, finally, by my own swipe at Rightist extremism.

By this time we knew our campaign was a huge success: our circulation was falling off like crazy.

"We're driving them away by the hundreds, Murray. We lost another fifty subscribers last month."

"Fantastic. Pretty soon we'll be down to eight or ten stalwarts. An even dozen purist middle-of-the-road anarchists firming up the center."

"The Galambosian is still hanging in there. He's getting better all the time."

"I don't know about him, he's a little too right wingy. Besides that, he's crazy. Gives me the creeps every time I see him."

"I'm keeping a close eye on him. He's not a bad guy, long as he keeps his mouth shut."

A Left-Right Festival of Mind Liberation was sponsored by the California Libertarian Alliance, featuring Leftists Paul Goodman and Carl Oglesby as well as spokesmen for the libertarian Right. Harvey Hukari, an ex-YAFer who admitted openly that profit was his supreme motivation in life, saw nothing wrong with informing on campus radicals to the FBI if the price was high enough. The warm response he received from the so-called Objectivist "anarchists" in the audience was a startling and horrifying experience for libertarians of the Left. Phillip Abbott Luce, formerly connected with the Maoist

Progressive Labor Party before turning informer for the Right, was also calling himself a "libertarian."

As was Jeffrey St. John, a conservative, pro-war journalist with Objectivist underpinnings, based in New York City. Just when we were starting to get something going, charlatans of every description were squirming out from under rocks. The people we'd left the Right Wing to get away from were now chasing after us, tracking us down in the streets to hop aboard our overburdened band wagon. The inclusion of people like Hukari, Luce, and St. John in libertarian ranks would inevitably destroy any potential Left-Right coalition in the gestation stage.

Next thing you knew, Lester Maddox and the Reverend Carl MacIntyre would be calling themselves libertarians. We had to squash them before they ruined us altogether.

In the spring of 1970, *Nation's Business* published an article in which libertarianism was identified as "the fastest-growing ideological movement on American campuses." Obviously, the piece would only serve to attract more deviationists to the fold. Just as obviously, we were waging an uphill battle. The more publicity we received, the more screwballs and oddballs would flock to our banner. It was a thoroughly demoralizing situation to be faced with.

And then, something happened which made us forget—temporarily, at least—our internal problems. Richard Nixon invaded Cambodia.

NIXON'S THE ONE!

That slogan was beginning to take on greater meaning every day. What could you do about a man like this? He had eked out a narrow victory in 1968, partly on the promise that he would get us out of Southeast Asia as soon as possible. You'd remembered what happened in 1952 when Eisenhower defeated Stevenson and managed to bring our involvement in Korea to an abrupt conclusion, and you'd naively thought history might repeat itself when Eisenhower's ex-Vice President assumed command. Why the hell else had you bothered to pull the Nixon lever in the polling booth?

Now here it was, almost a year and a half since he had taken office, and not only had the man made no real attempts to end the draft—another campaign pledge—but the war was actually being expanded under his administration. Whatever reasons he gave for the escalation, he clearly was still clinging to the old anti-Communist paranoia that had so influenced his politics from the late 1940's throughout the fifties. He just couldn't get it through his head that American "traditions" weren't being threatened here, that communism wasn't the monolithic bogeyman it was made out to be under John Foster Dulles, that in any case the peasants he was hell-bent on bombing out of existence were the greatest victims of the war, and not its progenitors.

Nixon, always fancying himself as a man of crisis (Six? Seven? How many?), saw himself rising to the national emergency and saving the country, possibly the entire globe, from extinction. Having lived in the shadows of other men all his life, he was determined at all costs to go down in the textbooks as a President who achieved greatness: Vietnam would be his Finest Hour, no matter what. Lincoln had his Emancipation Proclamation; John F. Kennedy had his Cuban Missile showdown; and Richard M. Nixon would be remembered as the man who brought us Peace with Honor in Vietnam. It wasn't enough for him to stop the damned war and bring the troops home, you see. It had to be done to coast-to-coast acclaim as the banner of Victory flew high.

For those of us who had supported him it was impossible to feel anything but disgust once we realized exactly what he was up to. For the country at large—Left, Right and in between—

it was a time of great despair, frustration, and then outrage with our own inadequacy, under a system of government theoretically set up of, by, and for the people, to do anything that would make him reverse course.

Not all the disgust was directed toward the mediocrity in the White House. *We* were the ones—the ones who had given this man more power than any other living human being on earth!

And here he was, raining bombs on people who were still living in a seventeenth-century agrarian society.

How much longer could we let him get away with it?

This was a time to put politics aside. Left? Right? Libertarian? The distinctions suddenly seemed unimportant. Only one thing mattered at this point: somehow or other the carnage had to be stopped. People everywhere, disgusted if not radicalized by this most recent escalation, felt compelled to make some gesture of protest against the war policies of the government.

I drove down to Washington for the demonstration against the Cambodian invasion, thinking all the while how nice it would be actually to lay hands on the man. How sweet to snap on the handcuffs and perform a citizen's arrest!

Was it not our right to apprehend those caught in the act of committing a criminal offense? Why should a criminal have immunity merely because he happened to be the President of the United States? No amount of votes in the world could give any man the authority to operate with the moral recklessness of a Raskolnikov.

I had heard in advance that government agents would be taking down the license numbers, for future surveillance, of all cars heading into D.C. Since I was driving a machine owned by an insurance company, my employer at the time, the idea of J. Edgar Hoover's lieutenants surrounding the main office in Hartford, Connecticut could only fill me with joy. Most likely the rumor was based on paranoia, but the spectacle of an upper-echelon crook in our state-corporate insurance system finding his house surrounded at three o'clock in the morning was a lovely one indeed.

Arriving in Washington in the late afternoon, I went directly to Karl Hess's houseboat on the Anacostia River. He had been living there with his girl friend over the past year, since abandoning his suits, ties, apartment, and all the trappings of his right-wing past.

The marina was a community of houseboat-dwellers inhabited by Hess, his son, and a wide assortment of their friends and disciples. Hess's leftward swing had continued on through syndicalism—which was where he was at during the October conference—and into the headier realm of anarcho-communism. He proudly referred to his waterfront group as his "little commune," and he wore his new mantle of voluntary collectivism as openly as he once had waved the banner of Goldwater conservatism.

Karl had split from the *Forum,* feeling that Rothbard's criticism of the radical Left was a bit too personal and directed more at him than anyone else. He was no longer interested in the concept of Left-Right coalitions, and since he was working exclusively with the Left, he felt that Rothbard's attack on the Left would undermine the overtures he was making in that direction.

Stepping aboard the "Tranquil," my eyes were drawn immediately to the wall poster of Che Guevara staring watchfully toward the deck. The bulkheads were papered with radical slogans and various kinds of revolutionary graffiti. Karl emerged from the vessel's dark interior dressed in heavy jeans and a denim jacket with the sleeves cut off, worn like a vest over a navy work shirt.

The look in his eyes cut me short. There was that glaze that had become so common with the kids of this latest generation, from love children to paranoiac Yippie subculturists.

Could it be? Had he actually opted for that route? What are you trying to prove, anyway?

Sure enough, the paranoia was there.

"Did you hear about the hardhats beating up the kids in Manhattan last week?" I asked.

"How do you *know* they're really workers?" came the unsmiling response.

Come on, now. Don't give me that nonsense, will you? That working-man-can-do-no-wrong line you used to laugh at two years ago. You don't really think J. Edgar Hoover infiltrated the trade unions with agents to create a pro-war demonstration, do you? Anybody who thinks that doesn't know the American working man from his Dutch uncle. I went to school with them, friend, I drank with them on weekends. You tell any self-respecting sheet-metal worker that it's O.K. to spit on the American flag, you just show him your Che poster and ask him what he thinks of it! You're lucky if he doesn't throw you into the Anacostia in your denim jacket with the red fist stenciled on the back.

How do I *know* those were really hardhats who beat up the dissenting students in the spring of 1970? Because I heard them *laughing* about it in the Blarney Stone the day after it happened; that's how I know.

We spent the rest of the evening in the boatyard watching Richard Nixon address the nation on television. From the way he moved his hands to emphasize a point; the way he flashed that toothy smile after delivering one of his deft witticisms; the way he furrowed his brow and stared directly into the camera when he told you how much he hated to kill people but how he had to do it to preserve the sacred institutions of the Western world; and the way his voice became low and solemn when he asked for the support and the prayers of his "fellow Americans"—you could tell that our leader was just oozing with sincerity.

"He's got to be removed," said Hess, glaring at the screen.

I had never believed in capital punishment, but I was almost willing to make an exception in Nixon's case. At the very least he should be traded to Hanoi—along with Johnson, Rusk, and a few others—for American POWs and have his fate decided by a North Vietnamese tribunal.

It was good to see that Karl's mind was still functioning clearly after all.

I got a few hours' sleep aboard someone's sailboat and rose early the next morning before anyone else was up. The river was gray and calm in the new dawn, and for a brief moment it was hard to see the filth and sewage that floated past the marina on its way to join the Potomac further south. The houseboats, side by side, bobbed quietly, almost in slow motion, on the gently heaving Anacostia. It was graveyard still out there on the catwalk reaching out over this strange river in Washington, D.C., with the boats rocking gently all around and not a flutter of human activity anywhere.

Driving through the early-morning streets of Washington, the only signs of life came from squads of patrolmen already anticipating the marchers that would appear over the next hour or so. Almost without realizing it I found myself heading for the Ambassador Hotel on K Street. This was my first visit to Washington since the summer of 1957 when I had been stationed at Quantico, Virginia, as a candidate for officer-training with the United States Marine Corps. The weekends, when I could get away, were invariably spent at the Ambassador in the company of a Mississippi honey blonde. How transient the nonessentials are—I had forgotten her name, but could still recall the drape of her silky hair across those smooth shoulders, the firmness of her stomach, the unsilky hair below. It was a fine summer if you counted the weekends and forgot about those long hours of brainless drill on the sun-bleached wasteland that was Quantico, Virginia.

On checking into the Ambassador I experienced for an instant the same kind of nostalgia that had engulfed me when I visited the Fordham campus after an absence of fifteen years. The corridors of this hotel, once crawling with Marines and other servicemen from nearby camps, were now teeming with long-hairs and blacks and others who had traveled from scattered regions to protest the war.

After breakfast I left and walked slowly down Sixteenth Street toward the triangular hub of the day's activities bounded by the Washington Monument on the south, the Lincoln Memorial on the west, and the huge field off the southern wall of the White House on the north. It was unreal watching thousands of marchers decked out in everything from business suits to beads and blue jeans, moving along the broad Washington streets in orderly fashion toward the meadow near the White House. The cops stood by nonchalantly, billy clubs and side arms well displayed, conversing easily with the wildest looking hippies from San Francisco and New York and all points in between.

Kids were smoking pot openly and the air was heavy with its cloying aroma. Patrolmen turned their heads the other way, apparently under orders to avoid confrontation at all costs and to react only to violence should it break out. At one point I saw a gang of Yippie and Weatherman types, their faces smeared with warpaint and FUCK NIXON spelled out in block letters on their foreheads, circling around a squad of police chanting "Off the Pigs! Off the Pigs!" The cops chatted among themselves or with other passers-by until the scurvy pack finally departed, ignored by all.

Dave Dellinger's voice, amplified through the speaker system, rang out across the meadow. The meadow itself was literally carpeted with people, contoured over the sloping grass as far as the eye could see. The sun raged high above, red and pulsating in the naked sky, making your shirt stick to your back and chest no matter how slowly you moved. After a while, when you'd had your fill of speeches and sun, you moved further south across another thoroughfare and up the grassy stretch toward the Washington Monument. Here, thousands more were lying about, eating their lunches on the grass, or turning on, or strumming guitars and entertaining one another with well-known songs or songs of their own creation.

An hour later, you left the vantage point of the Washington Monument with its bird's-eye view of the river to the south and the White House to the north, and you walked the quarter-mile or so to the Reflecting Pool in front of the Lincoln Memorial. Things were livelier here. Hundreds had stripped down to their skins and jumped into the cooling water of the pool. Dozens more were divesting themselves of shoes and pants and making ready to join the fun. A ring of cops stood in the shade along the grassy knoll to the sides, some observing the festivities with a grin, others looking on grim-mouthed behind the anonymity of their wraparound sunglasses.

The kids were circling bare-assed in the pool, sitting on the various jets of water and deflecting them toward the spectators on the perimeter. There were hefty Jewesses from Hunter College frolicking in the middle of the pool, their pendulous breasts flopping about like punching bags; there were scrawny college dropouts with boils on their backs and gigantic erections plowing through the water in a diligent search for receptive apertures. After a while, the grabbing and touching and groping was universal. By the time they started jumping up and down and splashing one another with water yelling, "One, two, three, four! We don't want your fucking war!" you began to tire of this a little and worked your way back to the crowded meadow and the speeches that were still droning on beneath the indomitable sun.

Later that night, high on grass yourself, you stared up at the Washington Monument, which shot like a streak into the pitch-black sky. It seemed to quiver with an inner life all its own out there in the blackness with the moon spilling silver all over its sleek sides. The air was thick and heavy with the sweet-sick smell of marijuana, by now a seemingly permanent admixture to the atmosphere. For a while you could enjoy your high and listen to the guitars and forget about the war and the killing and all the devastation it had wreaked on the lives of so many human beings, and on your country.

For a moment at least, out there near the Washington Monument, it was possible to get away from it.

The following morning, before you left the city that was the capital of your country, you read in the newspaper that Richard Nixon had made a personal appearance in the early dawn of the previous day, speaking to students near the Lincoln Memorial. Your biggest regret as you directed your car northward out of town was that not a single one of those students had the presence of mind to make a citizen's arrest; and you weren't there to do it yourself.

An opportunity such as that comes along only once in a lifetime, if ever it comes at all.

14

Left, Right, and In Between

"This is a movement to be proud of, Murray. A good, purist, middle-of-the-road revolutionary movement."

"All the crazies are gone for good. It's a nice feeling to know you can hold your head up high and call yourself an anarchist at the same time."

"No more crackpotism to worry about No more Neander-thalism. Murray, I haven't slept this well since Al Martino made a comeback in the middle sixties."

"All the weirdos have gone over to the extremists by now."

"You don't know how great it is to be able to finish a meal without running for the Bromo-Seltzer. My digestive juices are staging a comeback. By the way, what ever happened to Hamish Menzies?"

"I don't know, I'm a Bach man myself. How many copies of your book have been sold to date?"

My first book, *Radical Libertarianism,* had just been published. "Six or seven, last I heard. I don't have the exact figure yet."

"It's pushing up into two figures already. You don't know who these people are, do you?"

"No way of knowing. People can buy books all over the country without showing identification. You don't believe in registering books like guns, do you, so we'd have a record of who's reading what at any given time?"

"As an anarchist I'm opposed to all forms of licensing and registration. It's a dangerous practice. The authorities would be able to lay their hands on every book and magazine in the country any time they wanted to."

"Still, there should be some way of finding out who's reading my stuff. I'd like to know if it's getting into the wrong hands."

"Shouldn't be too big a problem if the book sells less than twenty copies. If the figure goes much higher than that, we may be in serious trouble."

"And we don't know who's passing the book around, either. Or who's reading my column in the *Forum* and passing *that* around. There should be some sort of rule keeping people who buy books and magazines from showing them to anyone else."

"Too Galambosian for me. We may have to get rid of him, by the way. His brand of heresy seems to be making inroads into the center."

"He's only free to talk about his modifications to Andy's system. Long as nobody knows what Andy's system is, we're safe."

"If you say so. You know, it's been a peaceful summer so far."

"It really has. I think we've finally got things under control, Murray. After years and years of struggle we seem to be on top of the situation once and for all."

It was hard to come up with an accurate estimate of how many individualist libertarians there were in the country at this time. The circulation of the most wide-ranging libertarian journals was somewhere around fifty thousand, but we knew that a sizable portion of these readers were really Buckley-style right wingers with a strong fondness for *economic* libertarianism, and political *conservatism* in other areas. Of the radical libertarian journals, all of which had purged any traces of conservatism from their pages, none was reaching more than ten- or fifteen thousand, at the outside. How many conservative hangers-on remained on those subscription lists was anybody's guess.

So far as active libertarian cadre were concerned, the leading organizations were the Radical Libertarian Alliance, the Objectivist-oriented Society for Individual Liberty, and a plethora of independent libertarian clubs operating on a local level. Both RLA and SIL counted their membership as ranging between five- and eight thousand but, again, no one could estimate the overlap. It is probably reasonable to assume that by the end of the summer of 1970 there were five thousand active libertarian radicals in the United States. About half that number were Leftist deviationists who followed Hess, while close to half were Rightist heretics under the influence of Ayn Rand and splinter groups in California.

Raising the banner of the moderate center were Rothbard and myself and a dozen or so middle-of-the-road anarchists whose task it was to hold the fringes in abeyance and keep the center from being overwhelmed. If we opened the floodgates too wide on either side, we'd be swept away in a tide of extremist propaganda. The price of freedom is eternal vigilance. We had worked too hard to lower our guard for a split second in these crucial late rounds.

Of course, like the lull before the storm, this state of affairs couldn't last indefinitely. It was only a question of time before somebody broke the dam and inundated us with problems once again.

The dam broke in the early fall of 1970.

Someone noticed us. Someone discovered us in our anonymity, in our saneness and our moderation, and began writing stories about us. They had gotten tired of writing about the Black Panthers and the Weathermen and the Chicago Seven. They needed copy and so they started to zero in on us. This could be disastrous. If they found out about our extremists we were finished—no group in the world had extremists like ours.

They found out. In September, *Esquire* ran an exposé of libertarian nomads and troglodytes—the ocean-platform claque and the cave dwellers. Stop it now, will you? We're responsible, we're middle-of-the-road anarchists. What do you want picking on a bunch of crazies like that? Have you no sense of proportion?

Then *National Review* blasted us from the Right, with a full-page attack on *Radical Libertarianism*. What are *they* making waves for, anyway? Ivy League Hegelianism is getting out of hand again. Who do you think you are, Bill, Jr.—H. L. Mencken?

Other right-wing journals fell immediately into line. First the *New Guard,* the YAF monthly, bombed our rightist flank; then *Triumph,* L. Brent Bozell's Sons of Thunder publication, dropped one on the radical center.

We had to consolidate our forces. The right-wing deviationists were being driven back to Buckley by the hundreds. They were exposed out there. They had no protection, no air cover, no nothing. We couldn't just abandon them, we had to take them back. There was always the danger that once they were back in the moderate radical center we'd never be able to get rid of them again. But we had no choice.

In November a surprising development took place. We suddenly found ourselves gaining support from an area where we least expected it: the liberal Left.

The assistance came in the form of a favorable article on free-market anarchism in the November 16 issue of *The Nation*. Can you beat that? *The Nation* found some kind things to say about free-market radicalism. The only problem was that they tied the individualist anarchist tradition to its European counterpart, anarcho-Bakuninism. Anarcho-collectivism. Anarcho-syndicalism. Wobblyism. Anarcho-communism. They saw individualist and collectivist libertarianism as cut from the same bolt of cloth. Total voluntarism was their line.

In effect, they had reunited the center with the fringes on the Left.

"It's a bloody Leftist avalanche. Everybody wants in now!"

"I can't stand it, Murray. My digestive system isn't strong enough."

"Next thing you know, Arthur Schlesinger and John Kenneth Galbraith will be embracing anarchism."

"At least we've got no appeal for Lawrence Welk or Bob Hope."

But all that was nothing compared to what happened when *The New York Times* decided it wanted in on the act.

Not *The New York Times*! Please! *The Nation, The New Republic,* the *Progressive,* even *Newsweek* I can handle. But once the *Times* starts in, you might as well put a lock on the door and close up shop. You'll never build a sane movement and keep out the crazies once you're discovered by *The New York Times*.

They started it with a December, 1970 article on Hess in the Sunday *Magazine* followed by a January issue with a cover story, no less: "The New Right Credo—Libertarianism." That one really did it.

Within days, I began to understand the charge that the New Left, the Black Panthers, Ecology, Women's Lib, whatever, are all creations of the media. In the brief span of five months, from September, 1970, through January, 1971, libertarianism emerged as the Movement of the Hour. From an underground discussion club comprising twelve moderates and five thousand deviationists, libertarianism had suddenly become a major political and philosophical force which threatened to sweep the nation off its feet.

Why were the liberals doing what they were doing? We didn't know at the time. Maybe they just wanted to embarrass William Buckley. Anyway, they did it. They made waves. Our center was inundated, not only with left- and right-wing deviationists but with legions of people who had never heard the word "libertarian" before *The New York Times* printed it.

They would come up to you with copies of the articles in their hands.

"Hey, man. What's this libertoonism I been readin' about? Sounds like an outasight philosophy, man."

"We been hearin' about this groovy new movement. How do we join?"

The New Left was floundering on the ropes. Women's lib was last year's issue. Ecology was being co-opted by the politicians. The anti-war movement was in a temporary state of limbo. These kids wanted a cause, any cause, to turn them on. They needed a movement. There was a vacuum to be filled and we were there at the right moment. The timing couldn't have been better had the whole production been staged by Cecil B. DeMille. Libertoonism was the Movement of the Hour.

"Where do we sign up for this outasight movement of yours?"

There is no movement, goddamnit! The movement has been disbanded. Go on home and do some reading if you're really interested. Try to find out why private property isn't theft. Don't take our word for it—convince yourself logically and then we'll talk. If you want to call yourself a libertarian, you've got to be able to defend certain positions that have been under attack from a hundred different quarters for a hundred years. You can't go around telling people that free trade and individualism are "groovy" and "outasight" and expect them to *believe* you. They'll just think you're un-American, some kind of Communist. Convince yourself and then come back. If you're really that interested when all the hullabaloo dies down, we'll be glad to talk to you.

By now we were engaged in some serious speculation as to why the liberals were showering us with so much convert-gaining publicity. The most obvious conclusion was that they saw libertarianism as a handy weapon to use against the conservatives, particularly at a time when a right-wing administration was in power. Divide and conquer.

But we were already divided, and had been, on a large scale, since the summer of 1969. True, giving national publicity to the fracture on the Right made the libertarian-conservative rift take on a broader meaning. It was easier to discredit the policies of a conservative administration when a large percentage of disillusioned right wingers were joining the attack.

Another possibility was that a major philosophical and political splintering on the Right just happened to make good copy. The whole idea of a group of free-market individualists and disaffiliated right wingers joining the radical Left on peace marches and anti-war demonstrations—all the while criticizing the domestic policies of the conservative establishment—was a fresh phenomenon in this era of polarization. It was a newsworthy development and may have been viewed as deserving of attention from that standpoint alone.

Then there was the undeniable fact that the liberals themselves were in poor enough shape politically to seek out allies and sympathizers wherever they could find them. As vulnerable as Nixon was, liberal Democrats were saddled with as sad a cast of characters as they'd ever been. It was almost as though the Republicans had selected their Presidential hopefuls for them. Muskie; Humphrey; Jackson, an old-time hawk who sometimes made Barry Goldwater sound like a peacenik; McGovern, the best of the lot from a libertarian point of view, but too low key to stir up enthusiasm—he had even less chance of making it all the way than Eugene McCarthy had; Ted Kennedy, somehow lacking the personal magnetism of his older brothers and, for the time being at least, still under the cloud of Chappaquiddick. At this point, libertarians had been making overtures to the Left for several years, especially since the traumatic break with YAF in the fall of 1969, and now that they had finally gotten a response they weren't quite sure what to make of it.

Tied in with this was the fact that the rhetoric of decentralization had suddenly become respectable again. During the years when liberals had been busy creating scientistic central planning boards in Washington, they'd had little patience with anyone who tried to tell them people had a right to run their own affairs. Decentralized power, particularly in the form of Old Right radical individualism, was quickly dismissed as "reactionary" or even "Neanderthal." But by the late 1960's, it had gotten through to all but the most stubborn of old-line liberals that their gargantuan technocratic machine in Washington somehow wasn't functioning properly. All of a sudden a new cast of characters was calling for decentralization and military isolation, the twin themes of the pre-Buckley Right. Now it was the radical Leftists who were criticizing their corporate-liberal mentors—their parents, in many instances—for having established a heavily centralized state which stripped individuals and localities of basic freedoms. Now it was Charles A. Reich—hardly a conservative by anybody's standards—who was lambasting the New Deal state-corporatism of Franklin D. Roosevelt in *The Greening of America*. Now it was Gabriel Kolko, another leading spokesman for the New Left intelligentsia, who was saying in *The Triumph of Conservatism* that it wasn't *laissez faire* but the state which had led to monopoly capitalism by the turn of the twentieth century. Now it was Norman Mailer, the Black Panthers, and a wide array of people with impeccable left-wing credentials who were calling for neighborhood government and local control of all basic institutions. Now it was *Times* columnist Tom Wicker who was writing about Left-Right coalitions in articles for *Playboy* magazine.

Suddenly, the basic tenets of libertarianism didn't frighten liberals so much anymore. How could libertarian principles be totally "reactionary" when some of the leading intellectuals of the radical Left were espousing them?

Whatever the motives behind the liberals' sudden publicizing of the libertarian cause, at least it was a beginning. An alliance of sorts, however shaky, was now a possibility for the first time in history.

The idea of a new political coalition is always intoxicating whenever it arises. As time passes and a society's political climate evolves from one stage to another, the shifting and realignment of various factions becomes all but inevitable. The old labels quickly become obsolete.

"Liberal" and "conservative" had certainly lost by 1970 the definitions they had in the early part of the decade. In the wake of the old divisions the distinction between centralist and decentralist was becoming more relevant. Totalitarianism and voluntarism were at polar ends of the political gamut; the choice between dictatorship and individual freedom was becoming more of a reality in the lives of all Americans now living in an increasingly polarized society with barricade situations erupting from day to day.

It is not surprising that, for many, these concerns should

take the form of choosing between an increasingly authoritarian government and the libertarian ethic.

What we needed to do now was to build libertarianism into an independent third force in American society. We had to set ourselves up in opposition to the centralizers, no matter what they called themselves. Anyone who wanted to accumulate more and more power in Washington was the enemy. The liberals would spend your money on public housing projects and welfare for the "needy"; the conservatives would spend it on "welfare" for the oil industry and the Pentagon. Liberal or conservative, it really didn't matter any more.

It didn't make any difference, because no matter who got into office it was all the same for the man paying the taxes. The only thing that could make a difference for *him* would be what libertarians were working for—decentralization and an end to the whole concept of nation-states.

Which meant an end to the particular nation-state in which all of us—liberals, conservatives, libertarians, whatever—were now living.

The Center Is
Big Enough for All

15

The Freedom Conspiracy at New York City's Columbia University was possibly the largest single libertarian chapter in the country. Surprisingly enough, the Conspiracy was also the largest student organization on campus—a novel situation for any group with libertarian underpinnings, and one which was unduplicated anywhere else in the nation so far as one could tell. If this could happen at Columbia, hardly a citadel of philosophical individualism, could West Point be far behind?

The first libertarian conference in 1971 was scheduled for the Weekend of March 13 at the Columbia University Law School. Its sponsors—in addition to the Freedom Conspiracy itself—were the Society for Individual Liberty and the New York Radical Libertarian Alliance. Conferences over the past year had included such Leftist spokesmen as Paul Goodman and Carl Oglesby; this one would be more individualist in orientation, with no spokesmen for the collectivist-anarchist point of view even invited to attend.

Before the conference began, word came down from Boston

155

that Noam Chomsky was concerned about the sudden burst of publicity surrounding the free-market libertarian movement. While he welcomed the libertarian-conservative split as a healthy development on the American political scene, he was apparently afraid we might succeed in toppling the federal government before Leftists could demolish the private-property system in the United States. Although we didn't share Chomsky's optimism about the imminent collapse of centralized government in America, we chose to interpret it as prophetic, and thus we were able to face the beginning of the conference in high spirits.

They paraded in from various corners of the country the way they had for the first gathering at the Hotel Diplomat. The same diverse types were here again, though hopefully, their penchant for extremist positions had been modified in the intervening year and a half. In addition to these we had managed to attract a group of Jeffersonian decentralists who journeyed by subway from Greenwich Village with a suitcase full of their own literature. All told, about three hundred and fifty Americans, and a few Canadians, came to Columbia University in March, 1971, to find out what was going on in the moderate anarchist center.

The Law School forum at Columbia University is large and bright and airy, in sharp contrast to the dark, narrow conference hall at the Hotel Diplomat. The crowd is orderly and quiet, with everyone in his seat well before the conference has officially begun. There is a soberness about the audience now that was lacking in the past, a reflective, open-minded mood in place of the raucous hostility that factionalized the first conference before it even got under way. There is another change too, subtle at first, but more and more discernible as your eyes sweep back and forth over the crowd.

The audience is integrated this time.

Whereas before it was compartmentalized into factions ranging from Leftist to the outer reaches of the Right, now you see random groupings all over the hall. Now you notice business suits and blue jeans, capitalists and communalists, pot-heads and martini guzzlers talking to each other, seated together throughout the conference hall.

The super-Randian is here, but no longer will he be selling black-and-gold whips in Times Square by the time he's thirty. Already he has modified his attire to a black jumpsuit over a gold turtle neck sweater, and while this may seem weird by conventional standards, it represents a marked change from midnight-black leotards and huge gold dollar signs.

Right on, young hero! You're doing just fine.

Missing, too, are the slogans and banners—the "Laissez Faire" and "Power to the People" and "Sock It to the State" clichés that characterized the first convention. Nowhere to be seen are the waving black flags and the clenched red fists of October, 1969. This time the slogans, fists, and dollar signs are limited to private lapel buttons, and that's something else to be grateful for. This is a time to collect your wits and reflect on what you are going to do. This is a time to figure out where the hell we go from here.

Now the moderator calls for order and introduces the first speaker of the day. You see him rising to address the crowd.

"Your theories on private judicial tribunals to replace the state law courts are very interesting, sir, but I don't see how they're going to work. Do you mind elaborating on that point a little more?"

Enough, I'm tired already of talking about private tribunals. I have to take a leak. Would you let me get off the stump for five minutes so I can go to the goddamn men's room?

"Your anarchist monetary philosophy sounds all right in the abstract. But before it will work in practice, you've got to do something about the international banking conspiracy."

Well, we know you, boy, don't we now? Our Man from Birch is here. Just *whom* are you referring to when you talk about banking conspiracies? You're not talking about Eskimos, I'm sure. No, there aren't too many Eskimos mixed up in banking circles. How about Venezuelans? Wrong again. Indonesians? I'm not even warm now, am I? I've got it. Corsicans! Everybody knows that the international banking community has all but been taken over by those sneaky Corsicans during the past two hundred years.

"Sir! Do you realize that at this very moment your life is in danger?"

Hold it now, pal. In danger from whom? From you, maybe? What are you talking about, anyway? You say I need an organization to help me hide out when the authorities come after me? What organization did you have in mind, friend? Anything I've heard of before? Oh, I see. Or, I will see if I just read this magazine called *American Opinion.* . . .

Infiltrated again! The center besieged by whim worshiping hair splitters, gray-flannel anti-Semites, and bearded Birch recruiters. What could we do about it? Purge? Purify? Drive out the deviationists?

As it turned out, the conference ended smoothly this time around. The deviationists proved to be a small—though unnerving—minority, while the center could now count a hell of a lot more moderates than ever before.

Sunday night we all departed in high spirits and with a feeling of togetherness. The various factions were still there, but for the first time they seemed willing to discuss differences in theory without flying at one another's throats.

And anyway, I was tired of worrying about deviationists. They can worry about me for a change. I'm not nuts, I'm a libertarian. A sane and moderate middle-of-the-road anarchist.

And I'm going to knock this government on its ass some day. Ragnar and I are going to blow the whole system sky high. Just like that! You wait and see.

PART FOUR

WHAT HAPPENS NOW?

An Optimistic Prophecy 16

There are several things that can happen now, and at this point any attempt at prediction is largely a matter of specula-tion. Still, there are certain trends and developments taking shape, and by analyzing them you can at least eliminate the less likely possibilities and come up with a pretty clear idea of what lies ahead for libertarians and for the radical move-ment in general.

So far as practical politics is concerned, there are two basic directions that any society may take at any given moment in history: it can edge further and further toward the totalitarian end of the spectrum until a condition of complete control by a ruling elite over the life of the general citizenry is finally attained; or it can slide the other way toward the anarchist, the libertarian, the non-state end of the spectrum until it approaches a condition of universal freedom through the ab-sence of control and authority.

In the former instance it makes no real difference in the life of the individual whether the total state is of the left- or right-wing variety—that is, whether the regime in power is recognized as Communist and nationalizes every conceivable area of human intercourse, or whether it is Fascist with state planners at the helm regulating the economic, social, spiritual, and cultural life of the people. The effect on the individual is the same, either way. There is a lack of options, a lack of alternatives, a lack of basic freedoms—freedom to speak one's mind openly, to write and publish openly, to associate voluntarily with others, to trade without interference in a fluid market place, to own material goods, to direct the course of one's own life.

Under communism the economic, social, cultural, and spiritual life of the people (if acknowledged at all) is nationalized; all institutions belong to the state—theoretically to everyone, consequently to no one except those in command. Individual freedom is not recognized and, in fact, the entire concept of individual rights is regarded as counter-revolutionary and detrimental to the life of the state. Which, of course, it is. The individual, his goals, his aspirations, his freedoms, are crushed under the absolute authority of the Communist state.

Under a Fascist dictatorship, a system of private ownership and private enterprise is sustained in name only. Actually the use of land, capital, industrial and natural resources, and other forms of "private" ownership are so completely managed by the state—through its systems of licensing, granting of monopolistic franchises, import-and-export restrictions, and other types of regulatory laws—that the effect is the same as outright nationalization. The life of the people is rigid and narrowly defined. The individual, again, is crushed under the authority of the Fascist state.

Here, at the polar realm of totalitarianism, Left-and-Right coalitions are a distinct possibility. The distinction between Left and Right is merely a distinction between the kinds of control the state will exercise over its citizenry; it is a distinction between total nationalization or total management as a means of maintaining absolute political authority. Left-wing and right-wing dictators are quite capable of entering into economic and military agreements with each other; Stalin and Hitler can agree to cooperate and recognize mutually exclusive spheres of influence as well as anyone else.

It should be clear by now that this is not what libertarians have in mind when they speak of Left-Right coalitions.

As we move along the political scale in the opposite direction, away from the totalitarian pole, we come to an area in which the United States finds itself today. It is my own contention that the U.S. has moved to a point roughly seventy-five per cent along the scale toward dictatorship, that we have been edging closer and closer toward this end for quite some time, and that we are continuing to do so at this moment in history. The total state toward which the United States is advancing seems to be of the right-wing variety, the Fascist variety for want of a better category, with the emphasis on management of private-interest groups rather than state nationalization. The "capitalist" system under so much attack from left-wing groups today is actually *state* capitalism, an economic system as far removed from the ideal of free-market capitalism as an equal degree of *state* socialism would be.

In this general area in which the United States is situated today, Left-Right coalitions are also a possibility. In the Congress of the United States we find a high degree of cooperation between left-wing liberals and right-wing conservatives, with each faction maneuvering for its own favorite kinds of legislation. Here the differences between Left and Right are differences between the kind of power Left and Right establishmentarians would like to see entrusted to the federal government. At this moment conservatives, whose chief concerns are morality and military power, want the federal government to legislate against "pornography," unconventional sex, abortion, political radicalism, and drugs; liberals would prefer the government to ease up in these areas and concentrate instead on assuming more power to deal with "social issues"—housing, poverty, hunger, education, and so on. There is also some indication that, economically, today's liberals would prefer nationalization of certain institutions rather than management of them, while conservatives prefer state-capitalist schemes like subsidies to failing corporations, licensing and franchise restrictions, import quotas, and anti-union legislation.

The primary goal of both, however, is a central state maintaining its present level of power under the absolute control of its own particular ruling elite. In other words, the kind of politics both sides are now playing will only serve to increase the authority of the state over the life of the individual, affecting in the final analysis only the coloration of the regime that eventually emerges as a left- or right-wing total state.

Again, this brand of state-corporate Left-Right alliance is obviously not what libertarians have in mind. Looking at the other alternative—a push further down the scale away from totalitarianism, away from the seventy-five per cent dictatorship we have already reached, toward the polar realm of libertarian voluntarism and universal freedom—we can envision coalition politics of a very different sort.

A society brought about through a libertarian coalition would be one in which those wedded to the Left, those wanting a collective life style with communal property and equal distribution of goods and wealth, would be free to establish their own communities or communes on a voluntary basis; while those on the Right, preferring private ownership of land and goods and competitive exchange in an unmanipulated market place, would be equally free to create their own institutions and communities. The ideal is for both factions, and all in between, to co-exist peacefully in a libertarian order of voluntary association, to leave one another alone without any faction's seeking to impose its way of life on another, hopefully to trade and communicate with one another, perhaps even to learn from one another and benefit from the experience of alternative life styles.

Granting this libertarian ideal, the problems currently standing in the way of its realization are monumental. There are times when the concept of an effective Left-Right libertarian coalition seems to be pure fantasy. There is resistance to the libertarian goal from, of course, the political authorities who must act to crush any movement which seeks to reduce their own power; from powerful private interest groups—oil, steel, trade unions, even the burgeoning welfare industry—which benefit directly from various forms of favoritism bestowed upon them by government legislators; from the middle-income class, both white- and blue-collar, which sees its own vested interests and standard of living as somehow tied in with the political *status quo,* and regards any attempt to upset that *status quo* with manifest hostility; from minority groups, notably blacks, Chicanos, and American Indians who have seen other voting blocs benefit from state largesse over the years and are now revving up their own organizations to demand a larger share of the state economic pie; and, perhaps most damaging of all, from libertarians themselves, both Left and Right, who refuse to work with other libertarian groups not in philosophical agreement with themselves.

There are left-wing libertarians adhering to Marxist economic principles who view all proponents of private property and free trade with supreme distrust, and consider free-market anarchism to be nothing more than a radical cover for incipient fascism; there are right-wing anarchists who regard any form of collectivism, including voluntary egalitarianism, as inherently totalitarian and refuse even to discuss differences of opinion with "irrational" and "immoral" collectivists.

There is also the danger that if, somehow, the radical move-

ment were to be successful and a genuine revolution were to
be carried out, Left and Right libertarians would wind up
battling each other for power; the winning faction creating
its own authoritarian state to suppress the "inherently totalitarian" opposition.

Discounting the sympathetic publicity in the liberal press,
it had always been the right-wing libertarians who courted the
radical Left. Murray Rothbard and Leonard Liggio, the first
to see the possibilities in a long-range Left-Right libertarian
coalition, had been calling for such a political readjustment
since the middle 1960's. Most of the radical conferences promoting the Left-Right theme in the last years of the decade
had been sponsored by right-wing libertarian groups.

So far, however, the call for an opening to the Left had
yet to draw a reciprocating gesture of camaraderie from leading figures on the libertarian Left. Since it was the Left that
had been the vanguard of the radical movement throughout
the 1960's, while the libertarian Right had only begun to
assume a radical anti-government posture in the last two years
of that decade, it was necessary for newly radicalized libertarian Rightists to continue seeking alliances on the Left wherever they could find them. The Left was where the action was,
so to speak; free-market libertarians had little more than an
organizational framework and a lot of publicity through the
spring of 1971, while the radical Left had put in a solid ten
years of on-the-job training in various forms of political resistance. If the Left had yet to respond to an appreciative
degree, it remained for the libertarian Right to continue the
courtship while it was still trying to develop a movement of
its own.

On a rainy Thursday night in the early part of April I went
off to address a class of left-wing anarchists at Hunter College

in New York City. It would be the first time I'd gone before such a group at its invitation.

Perhaps the whole thing might have come off a little better had I been alone. I don't know; it's easy to speculate with the benefit of hindsight. Anyway, there to lend me moral support was a grouplet of right-wing libertarians, including a radical Objectivist follower of Mary's, complete with lapel pins, LAISSEZ FAIRE buttons, and a whole grab bag stocked with right-wing bric-a-brac. While a classroom full of hairy anarcho-Communists sat around in their love beads, head bands, brocaded vests, and walrus mustaches, the anarcho-Objectivist set up shop in the corner selling capitalist literature and LAISSEZ FAIRE buttons at twenty-five cents a throw.

Somehow, I had this premonition that all might not go according to plan.

Beginning somewhat apprehensively, I emphasized the areas of agreement between free-market anarchists and anarchists of the Left. We were all against the war, against the draft, against the American state-corporate economic system, against legislation regulating sexual practices and abortions, against censorship of literature whether "pornographic" or not, and against any other curtailment of basic civil liberties; we were all in favor of local self-determination, control of civic institutions at the consumer rather than the managerial level, a maximum amount of individual freedom and expression.

So far so good.

The great barrier between us, of course, was the formulation of economic principles, most especially the question of property rights. Here you had to step a bit more carefully.

"Hey, man. What do you mean by free-market economics anyway?" a voice called out through a furry beard in the back of the room.

"Free exchange of goods and ideas on an open market place."

"You don't mean that if some pig wanted to own his own factory and hire other people to work for him, he could get away with that, do you, man?"

"The only way you can stop private ownership and the exchange of labor for capital is by state coercion. If you're serious about anarchism you have to accept the possibility of all forms of voluntary exchange whether you like them or not."

"Like, that's exploitation! How about private property, man? You don't believe in private property, do you?"

"There's no such thing as freedom without a private-property system. There's no way you can divide the earth equally among all people even if you wanted to."

"We don't wanta divide, man, we want everybody to use anything he needs. The earth belongs to everybody."

"It's impossible for everybody to use everything in common. Unless you acknowledge the concept of individual autonomy and individual ownership, there can be no freedom, no privacy."

"Fuck privacy, man! We all gotta love one another. I mean, like, we're all brothers, you know what I mean?"

"If some people want privacy, they have a right to it. You can't force people to share everything if they don't want to, not in a voluntary society. That's not anarchism, you need a dictatorship for that."

"You can't have some pig ripping off the land from the people and let him get away with it. That's exploitation, not freedom. Some greedy fuckers are gonna have more land and more money than others under your system."

"The only way you can guarantee complete economic equality is with a dictatorship. And if you destroy individual initiative, you'll only be able to guarantee equality at the lowest level. If you want to eliminate greed in a libertarian society, you have to do it through education—if you try to outlaw it you'll have to create a state all over again."

"GREED IS WHAT MAKES THE WORLD GO 'ROUND!" the radical Objectivist screamed, bringing the classroom to silence. "The profit motive is part of human nature. You people are denying human nature. A is A. A thing is what it is. You can't deny reality. Collectivism is a philosophy for psychotic, anti-life whim worshipers."

"Who is that creep anyway?"

"Like, what's he saying?"

"Who the fuck you talkin' to, baby?"

"I came here to hear a lecture tonight," the right-wing deviationist continued. "Why don't you have the courtesy to keep quiet until the speaker has finished his presentation?"

"He's a pig!"

"He's a goddamn male chauvinist!" shrieked a hefty feminist in the first row.

Now the Objectivist was on his feet.

"I just want to know one thing. If we were living in an anarchist society and you people had your commune organized the way you wanted it, what would you do about private-property owners who didn't threaten you in any way? Suppose there was a capitalist community five miles away that left you alone and minded its own business—would you co-exist with it or would you try to suppress it?"

Perhaps it was a reaction against the anarcho-capitalist and his little market place, perhaps they really meant it; I have no way of knowing for sure. But to this question there was a universal outcry from the class at large:

"We'd come in and kick shit out of you, man!"

"We'd beat your ass in!"

"We'd rip you off, baby! Just like that!"

I slowly started to gather my paraphernalia. The meeting was clearly out of control. By the time I left there were at least ten or twelve people standing on chairs, shaking their fists, and shrieking simultaneously at the top of their lungs.

Richard Nixon and Spiro Agnew had no reason to lose any sleep over us that night.

Nor did they several weeks later when a right-wing group at the State University of New York in Stony Brook, Long Island, invited me out to talk about the long-range possibilities for a Left-Right libertarian alliance.

I drove out on a Tuesday night and found myself overwhelmed by the bleak, Kafkaesque nightmare of the university grounds. You drove on through vast stretches of flat, undeveloped wasteland punctuated now and then by ultramodern dormitories or administration buildings rising in lonely isolation in the middle of nowhere. What an incredible waste of the taxpayers' money! Here was an enormous tract of land claimed by the state for purposes of education, its multimillion-dollar buildings scattered miles from one another. The very look of the place was the antithesis of Paul Goodman's concept of a "Community of Scholars." Students were trapped in expensive modern buildings styled like upper middle-class housing cooperatives, separated literally by miles from other student dorms and areas of cultural activity. There was more feeling of community in a prefabricated army barracks than you could ever find in a place like this. Ironically enough, the area I was headed for was Lenny Bruce College, a designation that would have caused the now-departed satirist to sue for libel.

The talk was scheduled for eight-thirty, and I found myself facing a group of students and some professors representing every conceivable point along the political spectrum. There was the leader of the campus YAF chapter with several of his membership; Objectivist anarchists who had invited me out; some middle-of-the-road Edmund Muskie types; a few Left-liberals in the vein of Eugene McCarthy and George McGovern; and radical Leftists under the influence of Mike Zweig, a syndicalist-anarchist who taught a course in economics at the university.

I started off with general principles, giving them basic libertarianism as concisely as I could, and then moved into practical alternatives such as police, courts, sanitation, education, and other institutions in a stateless society. It was interesting catching flak from all directions—Left, Right, and Center—at the same time. It was a lively group, imaginative and sharp and not unruly like the claque I'd faced at Hunter. After touching as many bases as I could and spending a solid two and a half hours on the stump, I finally prepared to leave. It was then, after all was said and done for the night, that I found myself confronted by several Objectivists with worried lines creasing their foreheads.

"How can we trust anybody who doesn't have a proper philosophical foundation for the concept of liberty?"

"Can we be sure of anything when we're dealing with people who fail to understand that A is A. . . ?"

". . . that a thing is what it is. . . ?"

". . . when you're dealing with people who are anti-life and anti-mind. . . ?"

At the first break in this flurry of questions, one of the Left-liberals interrupted to make her own point.

"You libertarians don't seem to be concerned enough about spastic children. How are you going to guarantee that spastic children and cripples will be provided for? How do we know they won't go starving in the streets under your system?"

"See what I mean?" said an Objectivist. "Left wingers are philosophical altruists."

"They're anti-self-esteem."

"All collectivists are inherent totalitarians under the surface. That's all there is to it."

"If *freedom* doesn't work, we're all doomed," was the best I could muster at that point. And so I left.

Much of the squabbling over property rights that always plagues attempts at dialogue between the Left and Right has come about because of the failure of many on the Right, including libertarians, to make a clear distinction between legitimate *private* property and monopolistic *corporate* property established with the help of the state. There is a world of difference between the type of property and wealth held by General Dynamics and Lockheed, for example, and a homeowner in Queens or North Dakota. The first involves state-corporate theft, the latter nonaggressive homesteading.

The property issue is crucial .and worth clarifving.

The right to land, whether privately or collectively owned, presupposes that it is acquired honestly and without force and that it is used in such a way as not to damage the person or property of others. In the libertarian view, only *people*—either individually or communally through some form of voluntary arrangement—can legitimately hold title to parcels of real estate. Since government is based on varying degrees of force—democratically, the force of the majority over the minority; dictatorially, the force of a ruling clique or party over the vast majority—it cannot own land under a natural-law theory.

While government claims to own land in the public interest, in reality it only holds land to serve the interests of the ruling class or certain groups favored for different reasons bv the ruling class. And since land claimed and neld through the coercion of the state involves the initiation of force by one group against another, even though it be *by* the majority *against* a small minority, government land as we have come to know it has no legitimate basis in a libertarian system. Government land, particularly federal land, can only exist so long as the people in power and those supporting them recognize it as a valid institution. Whenever a group in society begins to challenge the legitimacy of public property, the idea of government land held in the common interest of "all" is exposed as a myth.

The land-controversy issue has been created partly because of a political dialectic that is supported by both the left-wing and the right-wing mentality. Both sides have engaged in a war of opposites; the right wing standing firm in the cause of private property, the Left raising high the banner of communal property. Most groups on the far Left, notably the anarcho-communists, view private property as theft and regard the private-property system as intrinsically evil. The right wing sees any attempt to communalize land as the antithesis of man's nature as an acquisitive creature, and therefore destined to result in a struggle for power and, inevitably, a totalitarian state. Actually, the private *versus* communal property dialectic is an erroneous one; the real issue is one of morality—involving land acquisition, the use of land, and the way in which land titles are held.

The related question of man's relationship to his environment is a sensitive one inviting wide disagreement, not only between Left and Right, but within these two broad opposing camps. The privatists constantly haggle over how much real estate an individual can claim, with some people seeking to put a picket fence around the moon and some natural-law anarchists seeking to limit private land holdings to the amount an individual alters through labor. The Left runs the gamut from Democratic Socialists who would tolerate small, private, land holdings, taxed to the rafters, with large tracts owned in "common" by state authority; to anarcho-communists and rigid ecologists who see any alteration in the "natural balance of things" as an evil condition.

The monumental challenge is to arrive at some sort of land system flexible enough to accommodate everyone in the broad sweep from Left to Right. No one, of course, can be permitted to claim the state of Maine as his personal domain, and some domestic and commercial structures have to be erected on real estate if we are to have a civilized society (even an outhouse will change the ecological balance to some extent).

Land, just as much as air and water, exists in the natural scheme of things, and is just as necessary for the survival of human life. Man requires land on which to live, and since individual man shares this planet with some three and a half-billion others, his right to the land around him is intrinsically bound up with the rights of every other person.

Since it is impossible for everyone to use the most desirable land—the most fertile, the most scenic, the most temperate—the originals of our species turned at first to the land which was most accessible and claimed it as their own. There was an initial scramble for land because there was no way to apportion the most agreeable spots on earth equally among the multitudes. This condition exists today. If it were otherwise, ninety-nine per cent of the earth's population would be situated in land parcels along the Mediterranean coast, the Bay of Naples, the Caribbean, the coast of California, the shores of Australia. We can assume a few thousand or so eccentrics who would prefer to meditate in the middle of the Mojave Desert or on the ice floes of Antarctica, but most people surely would opt for their "fair share" of the choicest areas if this were at all feasible.

It is morally irrelevant whether, when man first began to claim the best available land for his own use, he did it individually—"private property"—or with a community of ape men whose society became a "commune." According to libertarian ethics, what *does* matter is that the individual or the community did not legitimately seize land which had already been claimed by others, and that the land claimed, individually or communally, did not exceed the amount able to be improved through their labor. It is not important when an individual or a small community occupies a plot the size of New

Hampshire if there is no one else around, and quite a different story when others are forced onto inadequate patches of dust where they can barely scrub out a marginal existence.

The other vital criterion for landholding and land use from an ethical viewpoint is that the land legitimately claimed by anyone not be used in such a way as to alter the person or property of others against their wishes. Here we run into the problem of pollution, which would be outlawed in a libertarian society as a physical aggression against the person or property of others.

Our old friend Ayn Rand has something to offer on the subject of pollution. On a Sunday afternoon in May, 1971, she appeared before a nation-wide television audience and denounced the ecology movement for being anti-life, anti-man, and anti-mind. Among other things she said it was a last-ditch effort to destroy what remained of the capitalist system.

I've long forgotten her actual words, but my supercharged memory and her position on the ecology movement would suggest something like this:

All of you out zere beyond ze age of twenty-nine should get down on your knees every time you zee a smokestack.

Ayn sweetheart, say you don't mean it. I know you can't mean what I just heard you say.

Pollution is ze symbol of human achievement. Wizzout technolochy and pollution, man would still be living in ze stone age.

Don't tell me fresh air and clean water are anti-life, Ayn. What kind of *rational double-think* is this?

Trees, rocks and mountains are nonproductive elements. Zey just sit zere occupying space, creating nozzing of zeir own.

But trees aren't very intelligent, Ayn. You can't expect them to produce a hell of a lot.

We are locked in a life-and-death struggle between nature

and technolochy, between mindless rocks and trees and ze boundless genius of ze human mind.

Forget this either-or crap, baby. Nature *and* technology. We can have both. We'll *recycle*. You know? Pump the filth back into production so it doesn't get into people's lungs. Pollution is an act of *aggression* for Christ's sake!

We'll build factories on ze beaches and highways over ze oceans. We'll build a smokestack to ze moon.

Ayn, you sweet, lovable, crazy bitch. Don't tell me it usually *ends* with you too!

Besides pollution, the question of how land is transferred is extremely important to the property issue. It is not necessary for people to "claim land in nature" in order to gain title to a chunk of real estate; the market provides for the transfer of property by peaceful and voluntary means—sale or gift for instance.

So far as the type of property existing in the United States today is concerned, it becomes apparent that neither "private property" nor "communal property" exist in the purest sense of the terms. We have a system in which state authority—theoretically the representatives of the majority—actually "owns" all the land in the country and leases part of it to various individuals, to corporations, and other organizations. Anyone who is under the delusion that he is the owner of the land on which he lives has merely to try withholding his "rent" from the government—rent in the form of property tax—and he will find out fast enough who exercises final authority over real estate in the United States.

It is almost impossible to determine accurately the legitimacy of every land title in this country. To do so would require a detailed search on every title, tracing back through the centuries to the point when the land was virgin. Libertarians would consider the most tenuous claims to be those vast tracts of land granted originally by the throne to favored families. Almost all of these, of course, have since been broken up and sold in parcels to private home-owners and municipalities.

Other titles which would be challenged in a libertarian society are large tracts of corporate property, much of which was seized from private citizens by the state and redeveloped for state-corporate interests; vast acreage in the Southwest and elsewhere, taken by force from the Chicanos and Indians who originally settled the land; former plantations in the South which should rightfully have passed on to the descendants of slaves who actually worked the land; enormous farms and ranches throughout the far- and Middle West lying idle while their owners collect hundreds of thousands of dollars a year from the federal government. (Many of these multi-millionaire country squires, collecting their own subsidy from the government, are quick to denounce "parasites" on the welfare rolls.)

According to a bulletin put out by the United Nations entitled "Progress in Land Reform," roughly half the land in the United States is owned by private citizens, while the other half is claimed by various levels of government. Some of this government land is maintained as forest preserves and parks which are open to the general public, and a libertarian society might turn these over to conservation groups which could certainly do a better job than the government does of protecting wildlife from the kind of vandalism that is taking place today. The great bulk of government land is simply sitting idle, unused by anyone; this would be considered open for homesteading in a libertarian society. As for those who are worried about the further development of natural land, there is nothing to prevent naturalists from claiming much of it and maintaining it as a natural preserve in addition to the ones that already exist.

Much thinking remains to be done if we are ever to resolve the private *versus* communal property dialectic that has dominated most Left-Right conferences until now. Both sides are going to have to re-evaluate their attitudes on the property question as well as other issues if there is ever to be a productive dialogue between libertarians of the Left and of the Right.

Having said all this we can now move into the realm of speculation. After weighing all the impediments to coalition, after considering the present dreary condition of society, after living with all the petty divisions and in-fighting within the radical movement, it is still possible to look to the future optimistically.

There are developments taking place in American society at this very moment which make it possible to expect that the current drift in the direction of a total state will soon be slowed and eventually reversed; that within the next few years American society will become looser and less regimented; that by the end of the 1970's we will be living in a less militarized and more decentralized atmosphere than exists today.

Our steady advance toward increasing state authoritarianism was made possible, primarily, by the sharp polarization between radical groups on the one hand—students, revolutionary Marxists, disenfranchised minorities—and, on the other, the gigantic middle class which comprises the great majority in our advanced technological economy. To the extent that the politicians could scapegoat these radical elements, particularly the blacks and the student militants of the far Left, making it appear to the law-abiding middle class that the radicals were responsible for the disturbing changes in American society, they could tighten their political stranglehold on the people with the support of a large majority of American voters. This is the condition that has existed in this country until the present time. The average American voter and taxpayer, feeling that his standard of living and everything else he held sacred was about to be yanked out from under him by bellicose left-wing radicals, chose to cast his lot with the government in every crisis situation that arose.

Unwittingly, the radicals assisted in this destructive polarization in the final years of the 1960's by their adoption of violent tactics when everything else had failed. If there is one thing the middle-class property owner fears more than anything else it is the specter of armed revolutionaries, particularly blacks, marching past his barbecue pit with reckless contempt for his life and property. In any confrontation between the radicals and the forces of "Law and Order," eighty per cent of the American people would opt for Law and Order every time. By condemning the middle class as "pigs," by showering contempt upon the institutions of private property and business activity, by "trashing" automobile windshields and other symbols of middle-class America, the radicals played into the hands of the politicians and their polarization strategy.

This state of affairs seems to be changing. Every day more "respectable" elements in society, including many established representatives of the liberal Left, are joining the radical movement. The violence of the far Left, so much in vogue during 1969 and 1970, seems to have been abandoned as a tactic by all except a small diehard minority. While acts of violence against the state may be morally justified in terms of basic self-defense, they have also been recognized as a tactic without a chance in the world of succeeding. The universal cry now is for nonviolent revolution, which is nothing more or less than massive civil disobedience, passive resistance, and refusal to cooperate with governmental authority in various areas.

In addition to the disgust and outrage generated by the continuation of the war and an aggressive American foreign policy, the middle class has now discovered economic grievances of its own: rising unemployment affecting a sizable percentage of the white-collar middle class; a high level of inflation, now virtually out of control; the devaluation of the American dollar; higher taxation on income, property, and luxury staples such as tobacco, alcohol, and gasoline; and a collapse in institutional services—education, police- and fire-protection, sanitation, housing, transportation, utilities, tele-communications—even as the tax schedule goes up. Because of this institutional breakdown, a lack of confidence in political institutions is affecting a larger number of people than ever before. More and more members of the law-abiding "silent majority," including such paragons of *status quo* America as policemen and firemen, are engaging in various forms of civil disobedience by ignoring court injunctions forbidding them to strike, by fighting for their property rights in cases of government condemnation of their land, by joining tax-resistance organizations.

A good example is the method adopted by an Italian-American community in Queens, New York, to defend their property rights against the Lindsay administration. Lindsay wanted to condemn sixty-nine private homes in their community and erect a public high school and an athletic field on the site. What made this issue even more outrageous than the usual destruction of homes for construction of institutions was the fact that, adjoining the private property, was the Rego-Forest Country Club, situated on *public* land. The members of this club live in high-rise, high-priced, upper middle-class apartment buildings in the nearby area. As such, they constitute a significant segment of Lindsay's over-all political base, and he was reluctant to tinker with the life style of his ardent supporters. It was easier to confiscate the homes of the Italian-Americans, who presumably would vote against him in the next election anyway.

Two community planning boards came out against the proposed demolition and submitted their findings to Lindsay, at which point the local Assemblyman, State Senator, and Con-gressional Representative tried to intercede with the city administration on behalf of the community residents. In addition to the private country club located on public land, they suggested a nearby public park and a run-down industrial site in the neighborhood as alternatives to the private homes. When all peaceful attempts to save their land had finally failed, the home-owners had two remaining alternatives: they could submit to city planners and allow their property to be bulldozed, or they could defend it by force.

Under the leadership of Vito Battista, a gutsy fighter for local self-determination, and with the support of popular columnists Jimmy Breslin and Pete Hamill, a delegation from the community stormed the steps of City Hall and gave notice that they refused to be moved. The rhetoric used was simple and direct—if the Mayor sent his demolition teams in, there would be an Italian-American revolution against the Lindsay regime in New York City. The outcome of this confrontation? It looks as though the residents will be allowed to keep their homes, and an alternative site will be chosen for the high school and athletic field.

The great lesson to be learned from this is that a group of middle-class Americans who had been among the most passionate supporters of "Law and Order," among the first to call for stringent police measures to save society from "un-American" activities—political dissent, black militancy, turning on, wearing long hair or Afros—suddenly found themselves "niggerized." These paragons of middle-class respectability—having achieved the world of manicured lawns and plastic slipcovers, having fought "for the flag" in World War II and also bragging, as New York's Mario Procaccino did, that not one of their nationality had ever been convicted as an American traitor (and Procaccino wonders why he lost the Jewish vote)—suddenly found themselves victimized by the system they had worked so hard to create. When the barricades were erected, they were willing to use revolutionary tactics to defend their own rights of local self-determination.

Just as libertarianism became "respectable" through the adoption of libertarian rhetoric by some spokesmen for the New Left, so the entire radical movement is becoming more respectable because of the growing number of Americans now willing to break the law in order to fight for self-determination. The tax-resisting middle American can no longer criticize the draft-dodging student for engaging in "un-American" activities; he can no longer afford to be self-righteous about others who refuse to "obey the law." More and more people are becoming "niggers" in our society. The cudgel of government is no longer wielded exclusively against blacks, students, or militant "undesirables." Everybody is fair game when the authorities act to maintain control, and awareness of that fact is radicalizing more and more people.

It is also true that the liberal establishment which controls so much of the nation's media is being forced—partly because of pressure from the far Left and the libertarian Right, partly because of an honest re-evaluation of its old bias in favor of centralized control—to take a more critical view of the kind of technocratic superstructure it is primarily responsible for bringing into existence. It is being forced to "liberalize" itself, to take a more tolerant view of the politics of decentralization, to give a wider hearing to other views besides the tired banter of the think-tank intelligentsia. In effect, the liberal establishment is being forced to loosen up, to give others wider access to the national communications network, to "decentralize" public opinion which could serve, over a period of time, to reverse our steady march toward the total state.

Most important of all is the impact that will be made by the generation of Americans now entering their early and middle teens. These kids have grown up in an atmosphere of political resistance and continuing social upheaval. Thanks to television, they have been exposed to the full pictorial horror of war, death, destruction, and every other form of human depravity from the day they reached the age of understanding. If we think we are witnessing war resistance today, it is tepid compared to the resistance that will take place later in the seventies if our current war policies are not reversed. Unless we are living under the threat of direct military attack from outside forces, young Americans in the late 1970's will refuse on a much grander scale than ever before to risk their lives in a senseless, adventuristic war. Theirs will be the generation of true internationalism—isolationism in military affairs; universal cooperation in areas of trade, travel, cultural and social intercourse. Having witnessed what their older brothers and sisters have gone through in the name of international power politics, they will refuse to put up with it themselves. They will negate the very concept of the nation-state.

And so we could be witnessing the beginning of a new coalition in American society. Ideological revolutionaries, radical students, and militant black power advocates are no longer alone in their struggle against the abuses of government. Disaffiliated libertarians from the Right have entered the breach in large numbers since 1969; left-wing liberals and Jeffersonian Democrats have grown increasingly radical in their own attitudes toward the arrogance of a centrally controlled society; and middle Americans, previously pro-Establishment for the most part, are showing a greater willingness to engage in illegal activities to redress their own particular economic grievances.

The aims of all these disparate elements differ widely, to be sure; but these people are united by a growing disgust against the war in Southeast Asia, and, hopefully, military hawkishness in general, and by a new awareness that they must take radical measures if they are to regain control over their lives.

The eventual success of the radical movement, in terms of actually reversing America's push toward the total state, depends to a large extent on middle-class cooperation. Middle America, comprising as it does the vast numerical majority in our society and contributing seventy-five per cent of the taxes which keep our state monolith in motion, can either "make the revolution" in a very real sense, or it can succeed in crushing it and ushering in a state of total repression. If the radicalization of the middle class continues, the politicians will have a great deal more to fear than they ever did from the blacks and the SDS; if the authorities succeed in co-opting middle America back into supporting a policy of politics-as-usual, or if the radicals manage to alienate the silent majority even more than they did in the late 1960's, a reversal of our present political situation will become all but impossible.

The greater danger, it seems to me, lies in the area of alienation. It is becoming more difficult for the political establishment to co-opt successfully. There is no permanent way of reducing inflation, short of embracing hard-money and free-market economic policies, and this is not likely to happen under either a conservative or a liberal administration. It is impossible for government to reduce the tax rate, or even to stabilize it at its present level, when more and more people are demanding better institutional services than are now provided by government. To improve the services it offers, government can either cut back on costs by firing civil employees—thereby increasing the unemployment rate among the middle class and driving ex-public employees to the welfare rolls—or increasing taxes to raise additional revenue, a measure which can only create further middle-class dissatisfaction. There are no other alternatives. And no matter which course it adopts, the government stands to lose power in the long run. If it decides to do nothing and try to preserve the *status quo,* this will only accelerate the state of institutional collapse we are already facing. If the middle class is again polarized to a position of hard-line establishmentarian politics, this condition will most likely come about through alienating tactics adopted by the radicals.

And this is the area in which libertarians could play the greatest role.

Within the radical alliance, the people who stand the best chance of appealing to middle-class interests and keeping middle Americans actively involved in radical politics are the free-market libertarians. The radical Left, with all its hairy-chested bravado regarding violent revolution, with its denunciation of private property and general business activity, with its destructive sloganeering about "pigs" and "Fascists" applied to anyone who prefers short hair and ties to jeans and medallions, can never expect to win the confidence of either the white- or blue-collar middle class. But libertarians—through their championship of the market place, of free enterprise, of the right to own private property; through their dedication to the ethic of individualism which is still very much a part of the American heritage, in fiction if not in actual practice—constitute the only organized group in the radical movement which could conceivably succeed in capturing the imagination of middle-class America. The great challenge that libertarians face in the remaining years of the 1970's is actually doing so.

There are a thousand obstacles that lie ahead, including several crucial ones.

There is the danger that a substantial number of libertarians may return to right-wing politics if the going gets too rough, or if they become too disillusioned with excesses committed by the radical Left. But the more time passes, the less likely this is to happen. The breach on the Right that has been created between libertarians and conservatives seems already too wide to be bridged; there have been too many nasty words exchanged, and too many basic differences in philosophy and politics which were never considered before have now surfaced.

There is the danger that libertarianism will lose its momentum as an organized movement and return to the obscurity and anonymity that characterized it until very recently. But, again, time is on our side. Libertarians are better organized and better financed now than at any time in the past; and the exposure that the libertarian movement will receive from this point onward, far exceeding the amount it has received before, will serve to increase the momentum.

A more likely danger: libertarianism could become factionalized and disoriented because of internal bickering over abstractions which probably seem unimportant to those outside the movement. The great strength of libertarianism lies in its flexible and nondoctrinaire principles based on individuality and nonaggression, and its innate ability to accommodate a wide range of attitudes and theories so long as they are noncoercive, but this advantage also constitutes its greatest potential weakness—a built-in Achilles heel. On the other hand, philosophical squabbles among Objectivists, natural-law anarchists, autarchists, Stirnerites, Galambosians, whatever, *could* strengthen the movement in the long run, give it greater flexibility and increase its ability to absorb other philosophies and styles of life which are also grounded in nonaggression. Certainly there is room for Quakerism, philosophical pacifism, Christian anarchism, the new Catholic resistance movement, Charles A. Reich's Consciousness III, and many other separate philosophies under the broad umbrella of basic libertarian principles.

All things considered, I'd say there is every reason to expect that libertarianism will continue to grow in scope and influence, staking out a permanent position of its own among other radical groups on the contemporary American scene. Libertarians will find their greatest areas of common interest with Jeffersonian Democrats and other political decentralists; possibly with Left-liberals of the Mark Hatfield or George

McGovern variety, who seem to be moving away from the state-corporatism of the New Deal-New Frontier-Great Society Democrats; with pacifists, anti-war, and anti-draft groups attracted to a neo-isolationist foreign policy; with middle-class tax resisters where, potentially, libertarians can have their greatest influence; and with various splinter organizations advocating civil disobedience and nonviolent resistance to government dictates.

Realistically, libertarians cannot hope to achieve their ideal of total voluntarism and total individual freedom within the foreseeable future, if ever. We have moved too far away from that concept over the past eighty years to see such a goal attained in one leap. But there should be no question that the path toward a voluntary society lies through the politics of radical decentralization. If we can succeed in breaking power down into small units; if we can succeed in reducing the level of decision-making authority to the state, to the city, further down into the neighborhoods; if we can succeed in creating even a partial condition of real Jeffersonian Democracy with moneys, decisions, and institutions controlled on a community level—from that point onward the ideal of pure individual freedom will no longer seem such a utopian pipe dream. The change would most likely take place in stages, step by step, level by level, over a period of years.

Libertarians will be channeling their energies into the three available means through which change can be achieved in any society—education, reform, and revolution. Education will continue through a steady flow of books, articles, essays, and radio-and-television exposure promoting the libertarian point of view. The tactic of education is vitally important; the more people there are in a society who understand a certain set of principles, the easier it is for those principles to become translated into concrete alternatives.

Education must continue, but by itself it is not enough.

Reform within the system must also continue at as fast a rate as possible. It is in the interest of us all to make life as pleasant as we can while we go about the business of establishing a freer society. Liberalized abortion laws, censorship laws, draft laws, tax laws, trade laws and sex laws are better than oppressive laws in all these areas.

The great danger of reform is that it tends to be co-optive—that is, it tends to defuse radical movements at critical points in history. Politicians never offer the people more than half of what they're looking for, and many of us are apt to shrug our shoulders with the attitude, "Well, what the hell! Half a loaf is better than none!" The danger of a liberalized draft law, for instance, is that it could weaken the push toward the ideal condition of *no* draft law at all. Still, reform can make life more pleasant, and co-optation, at best, is never more than temporary anyway. (Nixon succeeds in defusing the anti-war movement for three or six months at a time by bringing home *some* of the troops instead of *all* of them, but every act of co-optation has its backlash, and each backlash is invariably a bit sharper than the last.)

The major changes will come about through the use of revolutionary strategy, and this is the most valuable tactic of all so far as immediate change is concerned. Libertarians will continue their efforts in the realm of nonviolent revolution, concentrating most of their energies on the anti-draft and anti-tax issues, the two bête noires of right-wing libertarians. Potentially, tax resistance is the most effective means available to reduce the power of government, and the one feared the most by political authority. It is also the one tactic most likely to attract the interest of middle-class Americans over a sustained period, and it is valuable from that standpoint alone.

Tax resistance is also vitally important because it deprives government of the capital it needs to finance its own institutions. While it is true that the government can print more paper currency so long as it maintains a monopoly on the money supply, this would inevitably lead to the destruction of the state money system and the state's credit standing in the international market place. It would also bring about the destruction of the state-controlled and state-regulated economic structure. People would be forced to find a new medium of exchange as the state currency plummeted in value; in short, this could lead to the creation of a more stable and viable form of "people's money," probably gold- and silver-backed certificates, which would be more acceptable in world markets.

Looking at tax resistance in more immediate—and practical —terms:

Picture if you will the marvelous sight of working mothers all over the country, united in their efforts to deduct child-care expenditures as a "business expense" on their annual income-tax forms. (At least one working mother has already tried it.) The government would either have to accept this do-it-yourself reform as a *fait accompli* or take millions of women into court for tax evasion, a costly and chaotic undertaking.

Better yet, imagine wage earners from coast to coast, perhaps organized under the auspices of the National Taxpayers' Union (415 2nd St. N.E., Washington, D.C. 20002), listing two hundred million dependents on their withholding slips— or three and a half-billion for that matter.

Visualize the magnificent spectacle of hundreds of thousands of taxpayers simply *refusing to file* each year on the grounds that doing so is:

1) a violation of the Fourth Amendment to the Constitution which protects the citizenry from unreasonable search and seizure;

2) a violation of the Fifth Amendment to the Constitution which protects the individual from giving incriminating evidence against himself;

3) a violation of the Ninth Amendment to the Constitution

which protects the individual from doing anything at all he
doesn't believe in (according to that grand old anarchist,
Lysander Spooner, if the Ninth Amendment were properly
interpreted it would lead to the abolition of government itself);
and

4) a violation of the Supreme Court decision regarding the
so-called "Miranda warning," requiring government to inform
each citizen of his Constitutional rights before acting against
him.

And if all this isn't enough, imagine taxpayers across the
country quoting the first line of the Internal Revenue Service
Code of Ethics—the part where it says that the income tax
is based on the "voluntary compliance" of American citizens—
and then notifying the government that they choose not to
comply.

Oh yes, it does read that way; I didn't make it up.

It's so beautiful, for Christ's sake, I can't stand to think
about it any more.

And so we look to the future with guarded optimism. If the
readjustment that is presently taking place in American society,
if the growing coalition of dissatisfied factions and especially
the radicalization of a larger number of middle-class Americans
can be sustained, we can foresee the establishment of a radical
new direction in our political, economic, and social system during the rest of this decade and long into the future.

Of course, there are no guarantees.

Of course, something could happen next week, next month,
or next year which would accelerate our steady advance toward
a total police state in the United States of America.

Of course, the radical coalition could collapse and break
apart.

Of course, the silent majority of middle-class Americans could be polarized further in the direction of estab-

lishment politics, of resistance to the forces for change and decentralization.

Of course, there is no guarantee that we can ever succeed in eventually "libertarianizing" the society we live in.

But we have to continue to try and to take advantage of the opportunities available to us—whenever they become available.

A recent example took place in the early summer of 1971, when representatives of the leading libertarian organizations entered into a working coalition with leftist Allard Lowenstein's "Dump Nixon" campaign.

Senator Mark Hatfield, long identified with the liberal wing of the Republican Party, has lately expressed a strong interest in libertarian theory. Along with Senator George McGovern, he wrote an introduction to a book by Karl Hess and Thomas Reeves criticizing the military draft; he published an article in the Spring, 1971, issue of SIL's *Individualist* praising the economic theories of Murray Rothbard; and in later speeches he has quoted Rothbard while attacking our centrally controlled welfare system.

Other trends are surfacing. Congresswoman Bella Abzug's bill to make New York City the fifty-first state—an idea considered "kooky" when Norman Mailer pushed it in 1969—is another step in the right direction, and will be enthusiastically supported by libertarians. If New York City can secede from New York State, why not Greenwich Village from New York City? Why not Macdougal Street from the Village? Why not John Doe (John Galt?) from Macdougal Street?

The prospects are intoxicating. Ragnar, you crazy bastard! You may turn out to be a Jewish Mother with a New York accent.

In May, 1971, Meir Kahane's Jewish Defense League, Joseph Colombo's Italian-American Civil Rights League, and Thomas Matthews' National Economic Growth and Reconstruction Organization (NEGRO), three radical self-help groups, formed a political troika with potentially far-reaching social consequences.

All these bits and pieces are not conclusive by any means. But there they are, falling into place and establishing a direction that leads away from Washington, D.C. and into the neighborhoods. If that road can be paved even a short way, it will mean that much less destructive power in the world. The effort to reverse our march toward the total state will have been worthwhile indeed.

When the alternatives are slavery or freedom, it is in the interest of everyone to get on with the struggle.